OXFORD UNIVERSITY PRESS

Oxford London Glasgow New York Toronto
Delhi Bombay Calcutta Madras Karachi
Kuala Lumpur Singapore Hong Kong Tokyo
Nairobi Dar es Salaam Cape Town
Melbourne Auckland
and associates in
Beirut Berlin Ibadan Mexico City Nicosia

OXFORD is a trademark of Oxford University Press

National Library of Australia
Cataloguing-in-Publication data:

Dann, Max, 1955-
Going bananas.

For children.
ISBN 0 19 554460 9

I. Title.

A823'.3

Typeset by Bookset, Melbourne
Printed in Hong Kong
Published by Oxford University Press, 7 Bowen Crescent, Melbourne

This book was published with the assistance of
the Literature Board of the Australia Council.

1   A couple of spooks

HENRY AND BLANCHE Bailey are the creepiest pair in Yarraville. Maybe in all of Footscray as well.

I don't even like walking past their house. You never know when one of them is going to be out there, watching you. They do that a lot — just sit out on their front veranda, on a splintery old bench, not doing anything.

They watch everything. They don't talk, or wave, or smile, or say hello. They watch. They stare straight at you, as if you're in their way.

They're both about fifteen hundred years old, and they're brother and sister. He's so thin and bent over, it doesn't look like he's got a chest. If it weren't for his bones, there wouldn't be anything of him at all.

He wears the same old striped suit every time you see him. His face is always covered in bristles, his cheeks sucked way in, and his eyes look as if they're about to pop right out of his head. The first time I saw him I thought he was dead.

Blanche Bailey is probably spookier than him.

She wears old-fashioned dresses that are all too big for her. She's thinner than him. Her arms and legs stick out of her dresses like wire. And they've both got the same mean little mouths that never open.

Their house is a dirty, dark brown colour, and they have the lights turned on in the middle of the day, with the curtains mostly drawn.

The front yard is concrete, except for a strip of dirt near the fence with two or three bushes propped up on sticks that never seem to grow anything. Down one side is a gate. It's too high to see over, and too thick to see through. It's got a sign painted on it that says:

But the dog ran away a few years ago. Everyone knows that.

That's where Dusting and I were now, at the gate.

2   No gold here!

'I DON'T SEE any handle. Do you, Thesaurus?'

Handles? I wasn't looking for handles. I was looking for one of the Baileys to come sneaking out of some dark corner. It was so dark we could have walked right past them and not even have noticed.

'I'll give you a hoist over,' Dusting whispered.

'Why can't we just open it and walk through?'

I could tell I was nervous. My voice always squeaks when I'm nervous.

'Because there's no handle.'

'Then why can't I hoist you?'

'How are you going to hoist me up? Look at us, Thesaurus.'

I didn't need to. I already knew what we looked like. But he was right, I suppose. Dusting is twice as heavy as me. He's not fat, but he's solid. He's made out of square blocks — square shoulders, square head, square body. In the dark he looks like a brick column.

I leaned the shovel against the fence. Dusting made a stirrup out of his hands, and I put a foot

3

into them. His hands are big and square, too. They make good stirrups. Once I had my balance he jerked me up. I felt myself falling, and grabbed hold of him.

'Not my head, Thesaurus!'

'There's nothing else.'

'What about the gate, can't you lean against that or something?'

I did, and he hoisted me up until I could put a foot on one of his shoulders. He grunted.

'See anything yet?'

'Just gate,' I whispered back. 'I'll put my other foot up.'

'See if you can do it without kicking my ear off this time.'

I got my fingers around the top, and pulled myself up the rest of the way. I had both feet on his shoulders. I could see over now, down into the sideway. It was long and narrow. There was a whole pile of something down there shoved up against the fence.

'What are you doing up there? I'm not a ladder. Hurry up and get over!'

I pulled myself up, slid over the top on my stomach, then lowered myself. There were wooden struts on the other side that I could climb down on. I didn't waste any time standing around. I found the latch and snapped it open. The gate's hinges creaked.

Dusting squeezed through, and handed the shovels back to me. The sideway was full of old ice cream tins. Hundreds of them, all lined up and stacked on top of one another. The Baileys must have liked ice cream.

We passed a side door — a big, dark rectangle, pushed back into the house, with a couple of steps leading up to it. We ran out of the sideway and reached the backyard. There wasn't much in it, just a couple of lemon trees, a concrete path, clothes-line, and a shed down by the back fence. Dusting leaned back towards me.

'It's over there, beside the shed.'

He started padding across the grass, and I followed him. There was a loud *crash* half way across. It had been me. I'd dropped the shovels.

We stopped where we were, and listened. When nothing else happened, Dusting waved at me to hurry up.

'I don't know why you didn't just ring the doorbell in the first place,' he growled. 'It would have been quieter if we'd come blowing whistles.'

He knelt down on the ground, and put his ear to it.

'What are you doing?'

'Listening to the ground.'

He stood up, took a couple of steps to one side, and pointed.

'Okay, you can start there,' he said.

'What about you, aren't you digging?'

'Sure. But we can't both do it at the same time. We'll take it in turns. You dig first.'

My turn seemed to go on for hours. I must have dug a hole twenty-five metres deep. I was standing in it up past my knees before I finally found something. I tapped it. It sounded dull and solid.

'I'll take over now,' Dusting whispered.

He stepped in, and finished clearing the dirt away. He scooped out three shovel-loads, then got down on all fours and wiped the rest away with his hands. He stood up and stepped out.

'It's just a bit of pipe, Thesaurus. You're digging in the wrong place.'

'I was digging where you told me to!'

6

'No, I said over *here*.' He pointed to some spot I'd never seen before, a couple of steps to the right.

I started another hole over where he'd said. There was nothing there either. I must have dug for another hour, and all I found was clay. I dropped the shovel and sat down.

'I'm not digging any more. My hands are hurting, and anyway, there's no gold here!'

'All right, stop complaining. I'll finish your turn for you.' He picked up the shovel, and began digging a new hole.

'I thought you said you knew where it was. You told me it was only going to take us —'

'Sssssh! Did you hear that, Thesaurus?'

'Hear what?'

'That! What I just heard!'

I couldn't hear anything.

'There it is again!'

I heard something, too, that time. It was a scuffling noise, over by the fence behind us.

'What do you think you're doing?'

Whoever it was couldn't have been far away. I turned around slowly, but I couldn't make out anybody.

'Didn't you hear me? What are you two doing over there?'

I knew that voice. I was sure I knew that voice from somewhere.

3   Going swimming
(a few days before)

I NEVER SHOULD'VE gone down to the Footscray Baths. Things could have been all right if I hadn't. At least I would have missed Dusting.

He was already there when I arrived. He was at the pool practically every day, practising for his Senior Swimming Certificate.

'Hey, Thesaurus!' he yelled out when he saw me. There was no escaping now. 'Where have you been? I was looking for you yesterday.'

Yesterday was Saturday.

'I was visiting Max. He's got a broken arm.'

Funny about Dusting's hair. He was wet all over from being in the water, but his hair looked the same as when it was dry. It's sort of bristly and stiff, and stands straight up on his head. He was lying on his towel doing exercises. He was trying to wrap one leg at a time around his neck.

'How did Max break his arm?'

'He fell out of his bunk in the middle of the night, and landed on his elbow.'

'What a jerk! How could anybody break their arm just sleeping?'

He stuck his legs straight out in front, and started trying to make his head touch his knees.

'I've been wanting to see you,' he went on. 'I've figured out how to get rich. And I've decided to let you be my partner.'

I sat down next to him. There was no point in trying to run away now.

'I don't know if I want to be rich.'

'Are you kidding?' He made a big show of sighing. 'This is a big opportunity I'm offering you. You could even get to go on a holiday to Surfers Paradise, like you've always wanted. I could have asked anybody in Yarraville. I'm doing you a favour.'

'What do I have to do?'

'Hardly anything at all. Have you ever heard of gold divining?'

'What sort of gold is that?'

'It's not a sort of gold. It's a special way of finding it. I'd try and explain it to you if I thought you could understand, but you wouldn't, so I won't. It's got something to do with swinging a pendulum over a map. It only works if you've got the gift.'

'Gift?'

He leaned back on his elbows and said, 'I just discovered I'm psychic.'

'Psychic?'

'I only found out myself last week. I just happened to be looking through some of my

9

sister's things when I found a book called *Psychic Phenomena*. It had experiments to try. It said that if you swing a gold pendulum over a map, and then find gold, chances are you must be a psychic phenomenon. I am, because I found gold. In Yarraville! I used my mother's wedding ring and my brother's street directory.'

'You found gold! In Yarraville?'

'Well, are you in? We'll share whatever we find. Seventy-thirty.'

I was pretty sure I was the thirty.

'Maybe,' I said. 'I'll have to think about it—'

'I knew I could count on you, Thesaurus. All we have to do now is go and dig it up.'

'Where is it?' I was starting to get a little excited.

Dusting mumbled something, but I couldn't understand him. I had to lean over real close to hear him.

'Where?'

'The Baileys' place!' I stood up and sat down again, out of breath. 'Not me. I'm not going poking around at the Baileys', not in a thousand years.'

'Too late, Thesaurus. You already agreed.'

'I never agreed to anything.'

'You did. I just heard you.'

He stood up and started to concentrate on stretching. There were a few other kids beginning to arrive. They were mostly from our school, but it didn't matter if they weren't. Everybody knew who, and how tough, Dusting was.

That's why nobody sat near us. They were all heading over to the opposite side of the pool. Nobody swam near us, either. They'd all probably heard about how Dusting was practising rescuing people (it had something to do with his

Certificate). You didn't even need to be drowning, you could be just swimming along minding your own business, and he'd dive in and drag you to safety.

Millicent and her skinny friend, Avril, arrived. Millicent's usually pretty skinny too, unless she's standing next to Avril.

Millicent and me sit next to each other at school. She's not so bad. She lets me cheat off her sometimes. She's got this funny way of sticking her hair up in a pony-tail on the side of her head, just above her ear. Her hair is a dark brown colour, almost black. And her eyes are big, but not popping out like the Baileys' — just big and wide awake looking. And her teeth are the cleanest, whitest teeth I've ever seen. She must stand over the sink all night just scrubbing them.

Millicent and Avril were heading for the other side, too. It was starting to look crowded over there. Millicent waved at me, and I waved back.

'Do you have to do that, Thesaurus?'

'Do what?'

'Wave at that girl.'

'She waved first. I was just —'

'You've got all day in class to wave at each other. I don't know why you have to wait till you're with me to start doing it.'

'I was just being friendly,' I said.

Dusting sat back down again. He was talking to me while looking up at the diving board.

'It always starts off with a little wave, or a smile. I've seen it happen before. The next stage is talking. You'll run into her on the street one day and start talking. She'll offer to buy you an ice cream or something, and before you know what's happened, she'll be calling you by your first name, and hanging around twenty-four hours a day. It'll be you that starts buying the ice creams then. They might be stupid, but girls know what they're doing.'

Dusting isn't all that keen on girls. When Wendy Ballast went and sat at his desk with him at the beginning of the year, he payed her $8.75 to find someplace else.

'What gets me, Thesaurus,' he went on, 'is that they're not even good-looking. You'd think that since they're so stupid at everything else, at least they'd be spared looking so ugly as well. That's why they all mostly leave school as soon as they can, to get jobs. They need the money to pay for all the junk they need to put all over their faces. We wouldn't be able to look at them, otherwise.'

'You mean make-up?' I said.

He nodded his big head up and down.

'Every girl I've ever met has got a cupboard full of the stuff.'

I didn't know he'd met all that many.

'Do you think I'd be where I am today,' he added, 'if I'd made friends with some girl?'

'I don't suppose so,' I muttered.

Stupid Gilbert (who nobody likes much), dived into the pool on his stomach. He made a loud slapping noise, and almost emptied the pool. He was swimming backwards and forwards across the shallow end, showing off, except you could tell he was just walking himself across the tiles on the bottom. He'd stop and look over every so often to make sure Dusting wasn't on his way to rescue him.

Dusting didn't seem to have noticed him. He was looking at me.

'When are you going to get some new bathers, Thesaurus?'

He never failed. He'd said something about my bathers every summer for the last three years. And it wasn't just once, it was every time I wore them — the same black and white checked pair I'd had for years. (I've got some new ones now, though.) I knew those old ones looked stupid. I don't know why he had to keep on reminding me.

'Maybe Christmas,' I said.

'Well, now you won't have to wait.'

I knew what he was getting at.

'I'm not going anywhere near the Baileys' place,' I said, 'not for a thousand pairs of bathers.'

'You'll change your mind.'

'Not this time.' I was shaking my head from side to side.

He started to get up.

'I'll see you later, Thesaurus. I'll talk to you at school tomorrow about it. Gilbert looks like he might be in a bit of trouble over there.'

He was off, running for the pool. Gilbert was scrambling to get out in time, but he was way out in the middle.

I didn't hang around to watch. I'd seen Gilbert being saved by Dusting before, anyway.

4 Voices in the night

I MADE A point of trying not to bump into Dusting over the next few days at school, but it was pretty hard not to. We were in the same class, ate on the same seat, were partners in folk dancing; we even walked to school and back along the same streets. Every time he came up to talk I'd start choking, or make out I had a piece of stone in my eye, and rush off to the first-aid room. But it didn't make any difference. He woke me up a few nights later, anyway.

'Psssssssst!'

Nothing.

'Psssssssst!'

Still nothing.

'Thesaurus!'

I sat up, awake. There was somebody tapping at my window. It was Dusting.

'Open up!'

I went and opened the window.

'Do you know how long I've been out here, Thesaurus? Twenty-five minutes!'

It was five past one in the morning.

'Okay, let's go.'

'If you're talking about the Baileys' house, I'm not going.'

'You can't back out now, Thesaurus. Not after you said you would go. I'm counting on you. Besides, it's only going to take five minutes. All we have to do is walk in, pick it up, and walk out again. The old Baileys won't even have time to turn in their sleep.'

'If that's all we have to do. Promise?'

'That's all. No problems. I had one of my dreams about it.'

'A psychic dream?'

'I saw it all there. All the gold you could imagine. Buckets of it. And I saw exactly where it was.'

I got dressed and climbed out the window. You know the rest.

5   Back at the Baileys' place

I WAS SURE I knew that voice from somewhere.

'I never knew you were like *that*, Roger Thesaurus. I always figured Dusting was, but I didn't think you were creepy as well.'

It was Millicent! I'd turned around enough to see her now. She was standing up on the other side of the fence looking over. She went on talking.

'I always knew you were a bit funny for hang-ing around with Dusting. I mean, you can't go around with somebody like that and be com-pletely all right. But I never would have taken you for a pervert.'

Dusting came and stood beside me.

'Who's that?' he whispered.

'Millicent. You know, Millicent who sits next to me.'

'What's she talking about?'

'I'm talking about you two. I didn't know Roger was. I've always known you probably were, though.'

'Were what?'

'Peeping Toms. You know, perverts.'

Dusting turned to me.

'She must have followed us here!'

'I live here, barrel body. This is my house!'

'Why didn't you tell me *she* lived next door, Thesaurus?'

I didn't get a chance to answer. Millicent was talking again.

'They should lock people like you up.'

'We're not here to peep on you,' Dusting mumbled. 'What would we want to peep at you for?' Dusting mumbles quite a lot when he talks to girls.

'All right then, why are you here?'

We didn't answer. 'See? If you can't answer, that must be what you're doing here. I'll go and call my dad.' She started moving away.

'We're digging for gold!' I piped up.

She came back again.

'*Gold!*' She practically tore roofs off houses screaming it out.

'Can't you tell her to shut up, Thesaurus?'

'I don't know what you're worried about,' she added. 'You made so much noise coming down the sideway, I woke up to see where the carnival was.'

'We don't want to wake the Baileys,' I said.

'You're scared of them?'

'Of course we're not scared of them,' Dusting said. 'We just don't want to wake them.'

Millicent climbed up higher on the fence.

'Gee, you've really made a mess over there, haven't you? How much have you found?'

'Nothing,' Dusting growled. 'We keep getting interrupted.'

'Well, don't let me stop you. I'll just watch you from up here. How do you know there's gold there, anyway?'

'Dusting's psychic,' I said.

'Psychic! Peter Dusting psychic! I don't believe you.'

'It's true,' I said. 'He's been reading books about it. He can swing a piece of gold on a string over a map and figure out exactly where to find it.'

'Why don't you announce it on the radio, Thesaurus?'

'Okay,' Millicent said, 'cut me in for a third, and I won't tell.'

'We haven't found anything yet!' Dusting snapped.

I'd never seen him talk so long to a girl before. He was almost chatting.

'Come on, Thesaurus, pick up the shovels. We're leaving. I can't work with her there.'

'You're not going, are you?' Millicent asked.

I gathered up the shovels and we headed back down the sideway to home.

'We'll talk more about it tomorrow,' she said.

6   Tomorrow

DUSTING HAS THE squishiest things in his sandwiches for lunch. I always have to look the other
way while he eats.

I'd eaten my lunch at morning recess. I don't
get all that hungry an hour and a half after breakfast, but anything is better than trying to eat next
to somebody who's wolfing down sheep's brains
in breadcrumbs.

We were sitting on Dusting's bench (the best
one in the schoolyard). It was underneath a
shady tree, not too far from the taps, and faced
the shelter shed across the other side of the quadrangle. We could watch everyone else eat their
lunches. Nobody ever sat on it except for Dusting
and me. It was Dusting's bench, and everyone
knew it.

He finally finished his sandwiches. Now came
the bit where he rolls the paper bag into a tight
little ball, leans back, takes aim, and throws it at
the bin out on the quadrangle. Sometimes he gets
it in. Not this time, though.

Next came the cake. He always eats a squishy

cake after his squishy sandwiches, like a vanilla slice, or a cream bun.

At that moment, Avril came back from the shop and squeezed herself in with everybody else over in the shed. She was saving a seat for Millicent. You could tell by the way she had her lunch spread out on the space beside her. Millicent wasn't far behind. Instead of going over to Avril, she kept on walking. She came right over to where we were. Right up to us!

'Move up so I can sit down, will ya?'

Neither of us moved. I looked across at Dusting. He was so shocked he'd practically stopped chewing his cake. Millicent had on a badge. It said:

THE BEST MAN FOR THE JOB IS A WOMAN

I'd seen her wearing it before. It didn't make any sense to me. I'd asked her about it once, and she said it belonged to her little sister Bernice.

'If we're going to be partners, we've got a lot to talk about,' she said. 'All I want is a third, agreed? Good. Now the way I look at it, you were doing it all wrong last night —'

23

'I don't know what you're talking about,' Dusting said.

'Yes you do. Remember last night?'

'Last night? What about last night?'

'Okay. If that's the way you want it, I can wait another day. We can talk it over then.'

'There's nothing to talk about.'

'There will be tomorrow,' she said. Millicent left and went to sit next to Avril.

'What did she mean about tomorrow?' I asked.

'Nothing. She was just talking to show off her teeth. She won't remember our names tomorrow.'

'Well, what about the Baileys' place? We can't go back now, she'd spot us right away.'

'Forget about the Baileys' place. I've found somewhere else. It's so big we'll have to hire trucks to carry the gold away.'

Dusting didn't get a chance to tell me about his new discovery because Mrs Sweet had just wandered around from behind the main building. She's the meanest teacher in Melbourne.

She wears orthopaedic shoes, and expects everybody else to do the same. She doesn't even use toothpaste. She rinses her mouth out three times a day in salt water. She told us to do that, too. She's short and bony, and her face sticks out of her head like a wedge. She had on a floppy dress made out of tie-dyed hessian bags. There was so much of it you couldn't even tell she had arms.

She was strolling in criss-cross lines from one side of the yard to the other like a street-sweeping machine.

She passed the taps, the shelter shed, told a couple of kids off for running, then headed out on to the quadrangle. She stopped beside the bin.

'Who put this paper bag here?' She's got a real

high-pitched voice that makes it impossible to keep on talking. 'Does anybody know who put this paper bag here?' she screeched again.

'I do.'

It was Dusting! Confessing? I couldn't believe it.

'Yes, Mr Dusting. Who was it?'

'It was Gilbert Windsmith,' he said.

'*Gilbert Windsmith!* Come here at once and put this paper in the bin correctly!'

Sometimes I feel rotten just being a friend of Dusting's.

7 It's a deal

WE WERE LATE getting out to lunch the next day. Dusting was helping me get my locker door closed. It gets stuck all the time. We'd missed out on eight minutes of our lunchtime by the time we got it to shut. Everybody else was already outside.

We walked out, around past the end wall of the main building, and over to the bench.

The bench! Something terrible had happened to Dusting's bench. Millicent was sitting on it! Just sitting there, as if that was where she sat every day.

Dusting looked terrible. He looked as if he'd swallowed something he'd forgotten to chew first. The whole yard had gone quiet. All I could hear was Millicent eating. She always brings crunchy stuff for lunch, like celery, and dry biscuits.

Dusting was gripping on to his lunch so tightly I thought the paper bag was going to split. I followed him over.

'You're sitting out of bounds,' he growled.

Millicent didn't say anything straight away. First she fished around in her lunch-box for about half an hour looking for an apple. Then she looked at it for a while, polished it, bit it, and talked with her mouth full.

'You two were so late getting out I figured you'd gone home.'

'Well, we didn't. Thanks for minding the bench. You can go now.'

Dusting was being pretty polite really. Millicent finished chewing that mouthful, then stared at her apple again for a while longer. She took another bite, and started talking again.

'Read the paper yet?'

'What would I want to do that for?'

'Because you two are practically in it. Page three.'

She picked a newspaper off the seat beside her and gave it to Dusting to read. It was already opened up to page three. The headline said:

Martians in Yarraville?

There was a photo of old Henry and Blanche Bailey standing in front of the holes we'd dug. Underneath it said:

> Some time during the early hours of Wednesday morning, there was a mysterious occurrence in the backyard of Henry and Blanche Baileys' home. They woke to find three large holes beside their tool shed.
>
> For no apparent reason, the holes appeared some time between 11 p.m. on Tuesday night and 8 a.m. Wednesday morning.

28

When asked if he thought the holes could have been dug by a large dog, Mr Bailey seemed doubtful.

'No, it wasn't a dog,' he said. 'We haven't had a dog for some time now. I think it was probably aliens taking soil samples back to their ship.'

His sister Blanche disagreed. She claims they have been living on the edge of a sink-hole for some time.

However, the Council Engineer, Mr Holiday, has stated that there are no sink-holes in the local area.

Investigations will continue today.

'That's a great photo of the mess you made at the Baileys, don't you think?' Millicent asked. 'I was there when they took it. I helped the camera man. There were reporters and police trying to find out who did it. I didn't tell them anything, though I could have, since I was standing right in the middle of them.'

Dusting handed back the paper, and grunted something I couldn't make out.

'You could get into a lot of trouble if they found out,' she added. 'I told them I'd let them know if I heard anything. Well, it looks like I have to be in now, doesn't it?'

'All right,' Dusting muttered, 'I'll cut you in for a tenth.'

'I want a third, or else I squeal.'

'Squeal?'

'That's right. First I tell the police, and then I tell the Baileys.'

Dusting puckered up his lips the way he does when he's thinking.

'Okay, a third of what we get,' he said. There

was something funny about his voice.

'Shake,' said Millicent.

'Shake what?'

'What do you think, box body, hands!'

What a thing to say to Dusting!

'I haven't got any gloves. You'll have to shake with Thesaurus. Do you mind, Thesaurus?'

She held out her hand and I shook it. It was funny. It felt sort of smooth and cold, almost nice. To tell you the truth, I hadn't spent much time walking around shaking hands with girls. When I got mine back again it felt sticky and dirty. I hadn't noticed it till I'd felt Millicent's.

'It's a deal then,' she said.

'It's a deal.' Dusting turned to me. 'Come on, let's go find somewhere else to eat.'

'Aren't we going to sit here?'

'I'm not spoiling my lunch sitting next to her.'

'See ya later, partners.' Millicent really knew how to rub it in.

We went and found a place over by the oval, and sat down on some gravel. Dusting had been holding on to his sandwiches so tightly back there they came out of the bag looking like handle grips.

'Say, Dusting,' I said, 'have you ever held hands with a girl?'

'Do I look like I hold hands with girls?'

'Glenn Schmidt doesn't look like he does, but he does.'

'Schmidt's half blind. He can only see out of one eye.'

How about that? I'd never known. He was the best cricketer in school, too. But there was something else on my mind.

'If I'm getting thirty per cent,' I said, 'and you're getting seventy, how's Millicent going to get a third?'

'You're the one who shook hands with her,' he said.

'You mean *my* thirty! Millicent gets a third of *my* thirty?'

He didn't answer. He just went on eating his handle grips.

'But you told me to shake,' I said.

'I asked you if you minded. Nobody said you had to.'

I was down to twenty per cent, and we hadn't even seen any gold yet.

'Anyway, I've found somewhere so loaded with gold you won't even miss it. You know when Mrs Hodscone was talking about that excursion stuff the other day?'

Mrs Hodscone had come up with this idea of taking our class camping in the country for a couple of nights. She was always coming up with ideas like that.

'Remember what she said? About how we could all think of places to go, and then take a vote on it?'

I nodded.

'Well, I've decided where we'll go,' he said. 'Bridgewater. It's out near Bendigo. I was concentrating over my maps last night, and that's where it is.'

'I thought you said you dreamed about them!'

'Sometimes I dream, sometimes I just think. Stop talking to me while I'm trying to tell you something. There was an old miner who found a mountain of gold up there. He had so much of it he had to come down to the city to get help. But before he could get back up there, or tell anyone, he died. He choked to death on a fishbone. People have been going up there ever since trying to find it, and never have.'

'How are we going to find it if nobody else can?'

He shrugged. 'Probably none of them were psychic. I've pinpointed his shaft to within a mountain.'

'But what about everyone else?' I asked. 'What if they don't want to go there?'

'I've figured that out, too. I've got a plan. Do you want to hear it?'

I said no, but he told me anyway.

8 The payoff

THIS WAS DUSTING'S plan. First we had to write 'I want to go to Bridgewater' on thirty-eight separate pieces of paper. We had to make sure everyone in the class got one. Then we had to write the same thing on another thirty-eight little pieces of paper. That was to make certain everyone had two, in case they lost the first one.

The next bit was the hard part. We had to convince everybody that they wanted to go to Bridgewater. Millicent and me had to deal with the girls, while Dusting fixed it up with the boys.

Girls are a lot harder to talk to than boys. For instance, boys don't laugh at you the way girls do. I had to bribe them all. It cost me practically everything I owned. My fur hat went first, then my shuttle-cock set, my entire key collection, most of my marbles, three mouth organs, a pair of pants, my clock, and thirty-six comics.

It was easier for Dusting. It didn't cost him anything. He just promised the boys he'd leave them alone if they agreed, and they all did.

We got it done on time for Friday afternoon

when we had Mrs Hodscone for English. She's pretty old, and doesn't get around real well on account of a bad leg. But everybody likes her. She doesn't believe the whole world should be walking around wearing orthopaedic shoes, for one thing.

'Now, who's been thinking about suggestions for an excursion?' she asked.

Max was the only one who didn't put his arm up. It was still in plaster. She asked Wendy Ballast.

'I want to go to Bridgewater, Mrs Hodscone.'

Wendy Ballast had my shuttle-cock set. She'd been playing with it, too. She only lives a couple of houses down from me and I'd been listening to her banging away with it practically every minute since she got it.

'Yes, that could be considered,' Mrs Hodscone said. 'What about you, Gilbert, where would you like to go?'

'I want to go to Bridgewater, Mrs Hodscone.'

She asked eight more in the class, and they all said the same thing.

'Perhaps if I put the question another way,' Mrs Hodscone said. 'Is there anybody who *doesn't* want to go to Bridgewater?'

There was a minute or two of silence while everybody checked their pieces of paper. No, everybody wanted to go to Bridgewater.

It was settled. We'd be leaving next Wednesday morning on a bus. We would be spending Thursday and Friday nights there, and coming back on Saturday morning.

35

9   The worst bus trip of my life

THINGS WERE PRETTY quiet for the next few days. Dusting and I started eating our lunches down the oval every day. Max had to go to the dentist for three fillings, and burnt his tongue on the drill. My dog coughed up a piece of old bone about as big as the Footscray Baths. My dad cooked a meal he'd never tried before, and practically poisoned us. I lost four tennis balls down the drain outside my place, and my share of the gold dropped from twenty to fifteen percent. Millicent found out she was only getting a third of my third, and made me change it to half.

Wednesday morning finally came around. Four had dropped out. Forty of us were going on the excursion, including Mr Lipscombe, Ms Mitchell, and Mrs Sweet. Mrs Hodscone couldn't go because of her bad leg.

We had to stand in single file outside the bus and walk on alphabetically. I hate all that alphabetical stuff. With a last name like Thesaurus, the only one who comes after me is

Gilbert Windsmith, and he's not big company. I've been thinking of changing my name to Andrew Anthony.

By the time I got on the bus, there were only two seats left: one next to Max over the wheel up the back, and the other beside Mrs Sweet up the front. I left the one next to Mrs Sweet for Gilbert, and practically tripped over myself making it up to Max before he did.

I don't know why I bothered. Max was in a bad way. He's not all that hot on travelling. It's not just because he gets travel sick, he just doesn't like being away from home much. It interrupts his television serials. (He watches every serial on TV.) His mum had made him come this time, though. She said he needed to get away more.

'How's your broken arm, Max?' I looked to see if my signature was still on his plaster. It was.

'I feel rotten, Rog. I think my mum and dad want to kill me.' He had the window seat, only he'd stuck up a piece of cardboard over the glass so that he wouldn't have to look out. 'Would you send someone with a broken arm away camping if you didn't want to do away with them?'

'I guess not,' I said. I only wanted to know how his arm was.

'They're probably hoping complications will set in once we're clear of any doctors. My mum's been complaining about the laundry, says it isn't big enough. They're probably already clearing out my room. All they need to do is knock down one wall, and they could extend the laundry right through it.' The bus started and we pulled out into Powell street. 'I don't feel so good, Rog. How do I look?'

Max looked terrible. He'd gone paler than usual. You could hardly tell he had freckles any more. He pulled a paper bag out from between the little gap separating our seats. He had a whole wad of them stuffed down there.

It was the worst bus trip I've ever had. All I got to see was the aisle on one side, and Max on the other. He spent three hours staring into a paper bag waiting to be sick. He was doing a fantastic job of keeping his mind off it. We had to stop seven times so that he could get out and walk around a bit.

We were almost there when Max leaned over to Mr Lipscombe in the front and pointed to a little garage ahead.

'Again, Max? But we're practically there. Can't you hang on for a couple more kilometres?'

Max whispered something else.

'All right, all right. But be quick.'

Mr Lipscombe got the bus driver to stop at the garage, and told me to go with Max, in case he needed some help. Dusting came too, probably to stretch his legs. It must have been uncomfortable having to lie across the back seat by himself.

The three of us got off and walked around the

petrol pump (there was only one), and past a set of screen-wire doors that had KIOSK & SANDWICHES written across it. It wasn't much of a garage. It had a house tacked on behind, and the whole lot was only just a little bigger than the bus. It had been painted a pink colour a long time ago.

We went down one side and followed an arrow pointing to the toilets. Nobody from the bus could see us here. There was also a side door leading into the kiosk. Max pushed it open and went in.

'That's the wrong door,' Dusting said. 'The toilet is the next one.'

'I know,' Max said, 'but I just decided I'm hungry.'

We followed him in.

The kiosk had a big glass counter going all the way across, two small tables against the window, just enough room in between to stand, and an ancient poster peeling off the wall advertising holidays in Surfers Paradise. There was no sign of anybody. We stood facing the counter.

Down below, under the glass, there were a few opened boxes of lollies, and some lumpy square things. I bent down and pressed my face up against the glass for a closer look. They were sandwiches! There were eight of them, all different shapes. They looked like the sort of sandwiches Dusting makes.

We heard someone coming from out the back.

A short, round man with fat legs came shuffling through the licorice straps behind the counter.

He had on an overcoat. It was thirty-nine degrees, and he was dressed up in an overcoat! His face was even rounder than his body. He was smiling so hard his cheeks were blown up like halves of tennis balls. He had on round glasses, to go with his round face. They were so thick they

40

made his eyes look as big as dinner plates. I sort of liked him.

'Can I help you gentlemen?'

Max did the talking.

'I'd like a packet of Fantales, please, and a—'

'Sorry, I'm out of Fantales. The truck is late this week.' He was still smiling.

'Oh. Well, a packet of Minties then.'

He shook his head.

'Licorice allsorts?'

'Sorry, I'm out of them too.' He sounded more disappointed than Max.

'Jelly beans? Kool Mints? Salted peanuts? Butter Menthols?'

Ah! Something at last. He had Butter Menthols.

'I'll have eight packets of them, please,' Max said.

Max started emptying his pockets looking for money. I never thought one person could fit so much into just a couple of pockets. He was laying it all out on the counter top: a dog whistle, a couple of bits of string, a pocket-knife, five hankys, one yo-yo, some fluff, swap-cards, and a golf ball. Not much in the way of money, though.

'That's $3.60, thank you.'

'Say, Rog, I'm a bit short. Can you lend me, ummmm, $2.86?'

I dug out all the money I had, and started counting through it.

'Are you gentlemen staying, or just passing through?'

'We're camping,' Max said. 'Down at Wombat Flat, for a couple of nights.'

'It's a lovely spot down there. But be careful to stick to the tracks. Don't go wandering.' The old man bent over, and started fishing around for something behind the counter.

'Why?' Max asked. 'Are there snakes? I knew there'd be snakes.'

'Oh yes, there are plenty of snakes down there all right. But it's the caves you want to watch out for. This area is honeycombed with old shafts leading to caves, and caves leading to more old shafts. Most of them were so thoroughly worked they began connecting up with one another. One wrong step, and down you go. So many of them were never filled in properly.'

'Has anybody ever fallen in?'

'Occasionally.'

'What happened? Did they get back out again?'

'Some did.'

The old man found whatever it was he was looking for, and straightened up again. It was a big old brown paper bag. The bus driver tooted. Max threw the Butter Menthols into the bag, shoved his things back in his pockets, and we headed for the side door.

'I'll see you three fellows again. And remember, watch your step!'

We got back on the bus and into our seats, and nobody knew a thing.

A couple of minutes later we arrived at the campsite. It was only a few more bends further to the gravel turn off, and then down a little more to Wombat Flat.

Mrs Sweet had snored all the way there. All the way from Yarraville. She was still snoring even after we'd arrived and started pulling out our tents. Ms Mitchell woke her in the end. She had to; the bus driver wanted to go home. I don't blame him for not wanting to take her back with him. The way she snored, it'd be like driving around with a water buffalo in the back.

10   We're there!

WE WERE CAMPED beside a river. We could see we weren't the first people to ever arrive there, because there was lots of stuff there already: a few wooden seats, a tap, a fireplace, a table, and some funny-looking toilets. Apart from that, it was mostly just a big, clear space. There was a wall of trees surrounding us on three sides. They were real monsters, like buildings. They just stood there all day swishing against each other in the breeze. On the other side was river. The flat part we were on sloped away down to it.

It was two to a tent (they were pretty small). Me and Dusting were in one together. The girls camped on one side, and the boys on the other, in rows. Mrs Sweet got Gilbert to pitch hers right in the middle. I guess she wanted to make sure everybody stayed awake all night listening to her snore.

Once we had the tents up, she read us the rules:

NO LEAVING THE CLEARING

NO SWIMMING IN THE WATER

NO SITTING AROUND IN SOMEBODY ELSE'S TENT
NO LIGHTING OF FIRES
NO GETTING UP TOO EARLY
NO EATING BETWEEN MEALS
NO TALKING IN THE TENTS AT NIGHT
NO BEING SILLY
NO HANGING AROUND BESIDE THE RIVER
NO CLIMBING OF TREES
STAY AWAY FROM OLD MINE SHAFTS

There wasn't much left to do except sleeping and eating (at meal-times).

'How are we going to get the gold with all these rules?' I asked Dusting.

We'd been given the job of buttering the bread for everybody's lunch. Eighty-two slices!

'We'll sneak out some time when they're not watching.'

'When?' I asked. 'I have to know so I can tell Millicent.'

'Are you kidding, Thesaurus?'

He was really piling on the butter. He was slicing off slabs as thick as the bread.

'She's my partner,' I said. 'I have to tell her.'

'Tomorrow. I'll let you know tomorrow.'

'Where's the place? Are we close?'

'We're almost sitting on it, Thesaurus. It's just up river a bit.'

He finished one more slice. It had taken him

about ten minutes to do eight slices! I was on my forty-first already.

To tell you the truth, that first day wasn't much fun. We buttered, cleaned up, washed up, scrubbed down the fireplace, rinsed out the toilets, brushed away the leaves, and collected wood. By the time we finished everything, it was dark, and we were lying in our tents getting ready to go to sleep.

'Tomorrow's going to be different. Tomorrow'll be a cinch,' Dusting muttered. 'Tomorrow we'll have the whole day to —'

Then he fell asleep before I could find out.

11   The trouble with paper bags is —

DUSTING WAS RIGHT about one thing, tomorrow was different. It started off different, and just got more and more different.

To begin with, we had porridge for breakfast. I always have two pieces of toast with honey for breakfast. I never have porridge. I hate porridge. You can never get enough milk to go with it. First it turns to Clag, then about half way down it becomes concrete. By the time you get near the bottom, most of it is stuck to the bowl. We had to have it. It was Mrs Sweet's idea. She'd been eating it all her life, and said it was healthy.

I'm glad it was Gilbert and not me who had to wash up the bowls. He was scrubbing away at them for hours.

He missed the game of rounders. It wasn't much of a game, though. The ball kept on getting hit over in amongst the trees, and we ended up spending most of the time looking for it. The only really exciting part was near the end, when Millicent caught Dusting out. Dusting got so angry we lost the bat as well that time. He had to go and lie down in the tent for half an hour to cool down.

Dusting was looking at a map when I crawled in. I'd never seen anything like it before. There were no streets, roads or names, just a lot of lines and numbers twisting around and around. He'd drawn an X on one side of it.

'That's it,' he said. 'Just a bit of a walk up river, back past that garage. Two kilometres at the most.'

I was leaning over to have a better look when I heard footsteps outside, then a soft pat, pat, pat, against the wall of the tent. It was Max, knocking on our tent.

'Hey, Rog, I've got to see you. Can I come in? It's serious.'

'Who's that?' Dusting wanted to know.

'It's Max. He wants to come in.'

'This is a two-man tent, not Footscray Town Hall. There's no room.'

'He says it's serious.'

'All right, two minutes. Tell him he's got two minutes. It's hot enough in here with both of us breathing.'

Max climbed in, sat down, and pulled a paper bag out of his back pocket. It was the same one the man at the kiosk had given him the day before.

'I've got a big problem,' he said. He opened up the bag and tipped it upside down. Money started falling out. A hill of ten and twenty dollar notes. Dusting sat up.

'Three thousand, one hundred and ten dollars,' Max said. 'It was in the bottom of the bag, underneath the Butter Menthols.'

He started shovelling it back in with his good arm.

'That's over a thousand dollars each,' Dusting murmured.

'Have you told anybody yet?' I asked.

'Uh uh. I'd be murdered. I wasn't even sup-posed to have gone into the kiosk. Don't you remember, they had to stop the bus specially for me?'

'He's right,' Dusting said. 'They'd murder him for sure. The best thing to do is split it up and keep quiet.'

'It doesn't seem right to just keep it.'

'Max's right,' I said. 'It must belong to the old man. It wouldn't be right.'

'Do you suppose he knew he was giving it to me? He went to a lot of trouble to find this bag.'

'He sure did,' Dusting suggested. 'That's the way it looked to me.'

'It doesn't make sense,' I said. 'Why would he want to do that, when he didn't even know you?'

Max nodded. 'I suppose you're right.'

'You know what your trouble is?' Dusting started. 'You've got no ambition. Neither of you. You'll never get ahead. You get a once in a life-time chance, and all you can do is sit around saying it doesn't make sense. You'll both prob-ably grow up to be police officers and —'

We didn't get to hear the rest. Mrs Sweet called everybody for lunch.

12   Recreational activities

WE HAD SALAD rolls. That's what Mrs Sweet called them. Maybe hers was better than mine. The one I had was just a bit of lettuce and two pieces of cucumber. It wouldn't have been so bad if I didn't hate cucumber so much.

After we'd eaten, Mrs Sweet read to us from her timetable. It was time for recreational activities. Nobody knew what 'recreational activities' meant except for her. Whatever they were, we had the rest of the afternoon to do them in.

Dusting told me to tell Millicent to meet us at the two fallen logs, just outside the camping ground on the track up river.

'We can be there and back before dinner time,' he said.

Max called me to one side as I was walking back past to our tent. He was hiding behind a tree stump.

'I'm going back,' he said. 'It's the only thing I can do.'

'Back where?'

'To the garage. I'm taking back the money.'

'Now? By yourself? Can't you just mail it or something?'

'Don't know the address. I've got to get it back quickly. What happens if he finds it missing and comes down here looking for me? What if they think I pinched it? I've got to go. I've figured that if I go back along the river I can be there and back in two hours.'

'Do you know the way?'

'Sort of,' he said. 'But that's why I wanted to see you first. Could you mind this for me?' He handed me an envelope. 'It's my will. In case I don't make it back.' I didn't know he had anything worth giving away. 'You've got my armchair and the bunk.'

I'd seen his armchair. It had fallen apart months ago. It was in a thousand pieces in a cardboard box on top of his wardrobe. And his bunk was bolted to the wall. There was no way of getting it down without pulling the house to pieces first. I stuffed the will into my pocket. It didn't seem right, somehow, Max wandering off into the bush all by himself with a broken arm.

When I got to the fallen logs, Dusting and Millicent were already there. Dusting stood up when he saw me.

'What took you so long, Thesaurus? I thought you'd been bitten by a snake and died.' Then he noticed Max. 'What's *he* doing standing behind you?'

'Max has to take the money back to the garage,' I said. 'And since you said we had to go past it anyway, I thought he could walk with us.'

'Well he can't. This isn't a tour I'm running here, Thesaurus. It's bad enough having to drag a girl along. How are we supposed to sneak away if we take half the class with us?'

'I won't be any bother,' Max said. 'You can just drop me off at the garage and go on picking your flowers from there. I can get back by myself.'

Dusting made one of his ugly faces and pulled me over to one side.

'What's he talking about?'

'I told him we were going off to pick wild flowers,' I whispered back. 'I didn't think I should tell him about the gold.'

'*Flowers!* Why did it have to be *flowers?* Couldn't you have said soil samples, or rocks? Anything's better than *flowers.*'

'Sure you can come along,' Millicent was saying to Max. 'It'd be dumb to walk along by yourself when we're going anyway.'

Max started telling her all about the money and the old man, and we all set off on the track leading up river. Dusting walked a few metres ahead so he wouldn't have to hear it all again. He said it depressed him.

The track ran all over the place. One moment it would be zig-zagging between trees, then dipping down towards the river, then climbing away in amongst the trees again. We stepped over rocks, past toppled trees, under loose branches, around to the left, back to the right, up along a ledge, over a creek. Some parts were so overgrown it didn't even look much like a path.

It was beginning to feel cooler. The sky had filled up with clouds — deep, heavy grey clouds.

'Do you think it'll rain?' I asked.

'It feels like it will,' Millicent said.

'Maybe I should go back and get my raincoat.'

'Of course it's not going to rain,' Dusting broke in. 'You can still hear the birds singing. Birds never sing in the rain.'

'I've never heard of that,' Millicent said. 'You made that up.'

'All right, when was the last time you heard birds singing in the rain?'

'How can you hear them if it's raining?' Millicent asked.

'Stop asking me stupid questions. I'm trying to concentrate on where we're going.'

We crawled out of a bunch of thorny bushes and straightened up. We were beside a hollowed out tree stump. It had rotted inside and the wood had turned a flaky yellow colour. It was a lot like other tree stumps we'd seen. The only thing different about this one was we'd already gone past it ten minutes before.

'We're lost,' Millicent said. 'I knew this would

happen if we followed you.'

'Nobody begged you to come,' Dusting grunted.

'You should have given me the map. We'd have been there by now.'

Dusting bent over and spread the map out on the ground. Millicent kneeled down beside him.

'It's this way.'

'How can it be that way? We've just come from that way!'

'No we haven't, you're all mixed up. You're looking at it upside down. That's a valley. We haven't been to any valleys yet,' she said.

'That's not a valley. It's nothing like a stupid valley. It's a mountain.'

I spotted something up through the trees above us. I walked a few steps to get a better look. It was pink. It was the garage!

'I've found it,' I said. 'Look, up through the trees! The garage!'

'I knew we weren't too far from it,' Dusting said.

13   A dirty business

THE GARAGE WAS quiet, just like the last time we were there. Apart from a small commuter van parked to one side of the pump, there was no sign of any life.

It was windy now that we were out of the trees. It was blowing the dust in low, dirty circles around and around the garage. The clouds were coming in lower, too. The kiosk was so crammed with the four of us in there at once, we had to stand sideways at the counter. We waited, but the man didn't come out.

'Maybe he's in one of the back rooms?' Dusting said.

'Hello!' Max called out. 'Anybody there?'

Nobody answered.

I looked down into the glass counter. He'd sold one of his sandwiches. There were only seven left.

'Hello!' Max called again.

There was still no answer. The walls creaked from the wind. Something outside blew loose and rattled away. Something else banged shut.

'Let's try around the back,' Dusting said.

We stepped out into the daylight again, and walked around the side without the toilets. There was a row of fat green bushes running alongside the building and out of sight past the end of the house. There was a veranda out the back running all the way across from one side to the other. It was messed up with old crates and empty bottles, and covered over with creeping vine. We walked across it, and up to the back door.

Max knocked.

'Okay, that's long enough,' Dusting said. 'He isn't here. Let's go.'

We'd only just got there.

'But what am I going to do with the money?' Max moaned. 'I can't just leave it here.'

'Do what you like,' Dusting said. 'But I'm not hanging around waiting. Besides, I don't like this place. There's something funny about it. It's too quiet or something.'

'*Have you found it yet?*'

'Who said that?' Millicent asked.

It had been a man's voice coming from outside, behind us somewhere, on the other side of the creeper. We went and peeked out through it. There was a cleared backyard, heading down in the direction of the river. In it were a sprinkler, wheelbarrow, five or six fruit trees at the back, and a tall man in white coveralls. He was shovelling dirt into a long, trench-shaped hole.

Whoever he was, he hadn't heard us.

'No sign of it.'

That was a different voice. I spotted another man over on the far left-hand side. He was yelling across to the other one.

'I've been up and down here twenty times. Are you sure you couldn't see it up near the garage?'

'Positive.'

The one in the suit was walking alongside the shrubs on the opposite side, bending down and prodding them with a long pole as he went.

'Which one did you steal the money from, Max?' Millicent asked.

'Neither, and I didn't steal it. It was given to me.'

The man in the coveralls spoke again.

'At least we've got the worst job over and done with.' He went on shovelling as he talked.

'You should have spoken to the old codger first, asked him where he had it hidden.'

'I should have done a lot of things.'

The man in the suit gave one last stab at the ground with the pole. He left it half buried, and walked over to his friend.

'I didn't think we'd have this much trouble. A fifteen minute job, that's what it should have been. In and out, and back to the cricket.'

'It could be buried, ever thought of that?' the coveralls asked.

The other one shrugged.

'Beats me. How are you doing over there, got it lying down flat?'

'No worries.'

'Good.'

'What are they talking about?' I whispered. Nobody answered me.

'I say forget it,' the coveralls said. 'It's going to be dark soon. We can send one of the boys up on Monday to find it.'

'We're not leaving this job half finished, Jack. You know how I feel about messy work. We'll finish it under torch light if we have to.'

'Professionals,' Dusting muttered. 'We've got to get out of here,' he added. 'We'll head for the road.'

'The bushes would be better,' Millicent said. 'We could get through them to the other side and split up. We'd have more of a chance that way. They'd catch up with us on the road. They've got the van.'

Dusting and Millicent seemed to be having a private conversation. I couldn't understand what they were talking about.

'They must have done it for the money,' Dusting said.

'What money?' I asked.

'The old man's money,' he answered. 'The stuff in Max's back pocket. They must have known he had it. That's what they're searching for.'

'But what about the old man, where's he?'

'He's in the trench.'

'You mean that hole? Out there? They buried him?'

I looked across at Millicent, and she nodded. Max sat down on a wooden crate beside the back door.

'I should have stayed at home,' he muttered.

'They're coming up here!' Dusting whispered. 'They're coming to have another look around the garage.'

Dusting was the first to move, then Millicent. They were off the veranda and scrambling into the bushes beside the house. I was next, with Max behind me.

'Hey! What are you kids doing up there?'

They'd seen us!

The bushes were so thick and springy I had to swim my way through them. I turned to see where Max was. He was behind me, taking his time.

'Hey, hold on up there!'

I could see glimpses of the men running up towards us. Millicent broke through to the other side, and was running free, down in amongst the trees towards the river. I couldn't see Dusting anywhere. He was so far ahead he'd disappeared out of sight.

'Watch out for the fence!' Millicent yelled back to me.

What fence? All I could see were masses of green leaves. Oooooomph! I found the fence. I'd hit it. It was made of wire, but bush had grown around it and hidden it. There were three strands of wire running along, so I crouched down and eased my way through them.

'Wait for me!' Max called out. He was asking a lot. The men were just on the other side of the bushes now. They were shouting things, but I wasn't listening. Max reached the fence two or three years later. I held the wire apart while he put a leg through. He got the other one half through, and stopped.

'*Hurry up!*'

'My pants are stuck on the wire.'

I grabbed him by his good arm and jerked him free. His pants tore, he yelled, and then we were running down in the direction Millicent had taken. The trees were tall and straight, and easy to dodge. We kept on going until the shouts of the men faded away. We ran until my head pounded, my legs started to ache, and my side tightened up in a stitch. We ran until we couldn't take another step.

14   No pink pigs here

WE SAT DOWN, leaning back on a pair of gum trees. For a long time we didn't say anything; we were too busy trying to breathe. I was breathing in gasps and my chest was hurting. I tried shutting my eyes, but things were whizzing around inside there. I kept them open instead.

Max looked worse than I felt. His plaster was dirty, his sling was almost torn in half, he'd lost one of his slippers, his leg was scratched and bleeding from the fence, and he only had on a half a pair of pants.

'I'm bleeding!' he cried out.

It wasn't exactly a big cut. It looked more like a scratch to me.

'Try and forget about it,' I said.

'I can't forget about bleeding to death.'

'Well, just try to think about something else.'

'What?'

'Anything besides bleeding to death.'

He thought for a minute, then said, 'We've lost them for good now, haven't we? Dusting and Millicent, I mean.'

'We'll find them.'

As I spoke, there was a crack of thunder up in the mountains. It was close. I listened for birds singing, but I couldn't hear any.

'We're not going to make it back, are we. It's going to rain now, and things are just going to get worse.'

I was beginning to think I should have left Max back at the fence.

'If we don't drown, or get caught by those men,' he went on, 'then we'll probably die of starvation. We could eat berries, but they're mostly all poisonous. That is if we don't get attacked by wild pigs.'

'Wild pigs?'

'That's right. Not the little pink pigs they have on farms, but big bristly things with tusks.'

'Let's keep walking,' I said.

'All right, but there's not much use. We're only going to end up more lost than we are already.'

'I'm not lost,' I said. I was lying.

'You aren't?' He sounded impressed.

I helped him up on to his feet. We kept on going in the same direction, veering right and walking alongside the slope. I had a feeling the river was below us someplace, so I got us to walk in a big circle. That way we could stay in the same area. And while Max was walking, he wasn't talking.

We climbed up, and then down again into a

shallow bowl. The trees began to group closer together. The ground underneath thickened up with old branches, bracken, and a blanket of leaves. We sank up to our knees as we walked. Every time I took a step, my feet would disappear from view. Max had dropped back behind.

I stopped. I thought I heard someone talking. When I didn't hear it again, I kept on going.

There was a tree lying across the ground up ahead, and a little further on, a sharp step up. I stepped over the tree, ran across the next bit, and made it up in one leap. I turned around to wave to Max, took another step, and ooooooh! I'd stepped into mid air. There was nothing underneath me. My feet hit something a moment later, but whatever it was collapsed. My legs buckled, I fell hard on my side, twisted, and rolled over.

I was caught in something soft. I reached back to free my leg. It had got bent up under my stomach somehow. But it wasn't *my* leg!

'Get off me! Get off!'

It was Dusting's leg!

'Will you get off me, you idiot!'

I untangled myself. Millicent was helping me to get up.

'What's the matter with you, Thesaurus? Are you blind, or just stupid?'

Dusting got up, rubbing his shoulder. We were in a pit. It must have been six metres deep and three or four metres across. The sides ran straight up, while the floor angled down on one side and finished in a low, shallow burrow tunnelled in about an arm's length. It looked about big enough for one person to crouch inside.

'What is it about you, Thesaurus? What did you do, stand up there and take aim?'

'I'm sorry,' I said, 'I didn't see the hole.'

'How could you miss it? It's as big as a football field.'

'I'm sorry,' I said again.

'You could have killed me. Don't bother apologizing or anything.'

'Are you okay, Rog?' Millicent asked.

'I think so.' I felt a bit shaken up, though.

'Of course he's all right,' Dusting said. 'He had me to land on. I'm the one who almost got killed.'

'What are you doing down here?' I asked.

'I was following Dusting, and he ran straight into it. I could have missed it if he'd given me some warning.'

'That's not the way it happened,' Dusting broke in. 'She started falling in, saw me going past, and reached over and pulled me down with her.'

'Why would I want to drag you down here with me?'

'How should I know? You were scared, I suppose.'

'Nothing is that scary.'

A bit of time alone together had really done

them some good. They seemed to be talking a lot
more to each other now.

Max finally made it over. He knelt, and peered
down over the edge at us.

'How do I get down?' he asked.

15 Strangers in the night

'WE'RE STUCK DOWN here. You're our only hope,' Millicent said to Max. 'You'll have to get help.'

'You're really stuck down there? All of you?'

'Well we're not down here to play tennis,' Dusting grumbled.

'I don't want to go to get help. I'd rather be down there with all of you. Maybe somebody will just walk by.'

'You've got to go, Max.'

'What about my broken arm? And I'm bleeding. Didn't Roger tell you I'm bleeding to death? I almost lost my leg on the wire fence.'

'It'll be dark soon, Max.'

'But I don't know the way back by myself. I don't even know where I am.'

'You're just down from the garage,' Dusting said. 'You see those two trees criss-crossing each other just down on your left?'

'No.'

'Well, you go past them, turn right up hill a little, then you should find a clearing with a lot of prickly bushes.'

'Snakes like prickly bushes.'

'Then you'll find a clearing —'

'What does it look like?'

'It doesn't look like anything. There's nothing there to see. After that, you go straight down till you come to the river, and follow it downstream to camp. You got that?'

'I don't know.' He took one final, long look down at us, as if he were lining us all up for a photo. 'I suppose I have to go, don't I?'

We didn't say anything. He stood up and left.

We'd only just sat down to wait when a spot of water hit me in the face. There was another one, then a couple more. I looked up, and caught one in the eye. These weren't just little drops of rain. You could've played golf with them. A streak of lightning shot down and split the sky in two. The sky lit up in a flash of yellow, and a moment later it began to rain.

Dusting reached inside his shirt, pulled out a small parcel and unrolled it. It was a raincoat! He'd brought along a raincoat! And a cap! He put it on over his clothes, and sat down again.

He was just in time. A minute later it began to pour. Water started streaming down the sides and making puddles at our feet. The ground had turned to mud. My clothes were soppy and cling-ing to me. Millicent wasn't too badly off, because she was huddling inside the burrow. I was the only one who didn't have anything to protect me.

69

'Can I have a lend of your cap?' I shouted across to Dusting. I didn't think he'd mind since he had the coat as well.

'Are you kidding?' he shouted back. We had to shout to hear ourselves over the rain. 'What'd be the use of having a coat without the cap?'

'Well, what about the coat then? Just for a couple of minutes?'

'I didn't carry it around all day just to give it away when it started raining. You should've brought your own.'

'I didn't know it was going to rain,' I said.

'Then you should've asked me. I would have told you.'

I glanced across to see what Millicent was doing. She'd disappeared! I crawled over to where I'd last seen her. The burrow went in deeper than I thought. I stuck my head in and called out to her.

'Millicent!'

'In here. I'm in here.'

I could hear her, but I couldn't see her. There was an opening there, so I got down on my stomach and crawled in a little further. There was dry earth under my fingers. It was very low and I had to squeeze my way in. Tiny landslides of dirt broke free around my head. I kept on pushing my way along until my whole body was in. I bumped into Millicent.

'What happened?'

'I don't know. I was pushing up against the dirt and it just gave way. The rain must have weakened it.'

I felt around and found a level place to sit.

'It doesn't just stop here, either,' she said. 'It goes on further, I think.'

'How far?'

'Can't tell.'

Dusting came bustling his way down.

'Are you two in here?' He slid into my back. 'Who's that?'

'It's me,' I said. 'You can sit up in here.'

'Not with you blocking the entrance I can't.'

I moved my way across, hit my head on something, bumped into Millicent again, and found somewhere else to sit.

Once we were all settled, we sat and just listened to the rain. There was nothing else to do. It was really coming down out there. It sounded like thousands of horses going overhead in slippers. I was beginning to shiver from the cold. My clothes were heavy and soggy with water. They were sticking to me.

'How far do you suppose Max has got?' I asked.

'He's probably still looking for the trees crisscrossing,' Dusting said. 'They'll probably find him still wandering about in twenty-five years, over in South Australia somewhere.'

'It'll only be because of the stupid directions

you gave him,' Millicent said.

'What was wrong with my directions?'

'They led straight back to the garage. It took me a while to figure them out, but that's where you sent him.'

'Well, you figured it wrong. If he goes the way I told him to, he'll be back soon with help.'

They stopped talking for a while. I could hear Dusting rustling around inside his raincoat.

Click!

He had a torch in his hand.

'I didn't know you had a torch.'

'Why didn't you use it before?' Millicent asked.

'Because I didn't feel like it. Besides, batteries are expensive. They don't just give them away, you know.'

'What's the use of having a torch if you don't use it in the dark?'

'I'm using it now, aren't I?'

It wasn't much of a torch, anyway. It was nearly as small as a pen, so it couldn't have cost all that much to run. It shone in his hand like a shiny button. If he moved it around slowly, we could make out most of where we were. The part we were in was only a couple of metres across and about a metre high. It sloped slowly downwards, further than the torch could reach.

I heard something besides rain outside. Voices! It was Max!

'They're down there!' he was shouting. 'Down that hole. That's where I left them!'

He'd brought back help. He sure had been quick getting to the camp and back. He must have run all the way. Dusting scuttled across to the entrance and lay down on his stomach. He started crawling back out.

'Last one out's got a face like a chewed Mintie!' (That was one of his sayings.) He was half way back up by the time me and Millicent had found our way across.

'They must be down there somewhere!' Max shouted. 'That's where I left them.'

There were other voices dancing around his. Some of them were coming from just outside, in the pit.

'Maybe they crawled in here. Hang on to this while I have a look.'

I'd heard that voice somewhere before. I had it! It belonged to the man in the white coveralls! What was he doing out there? And who were all the others? They must have had a whole gang out there with them.

'I'll poke my head in and have a look,' he added.

'They've caught Max,' Millicent whispered.

Then Dusting started kicking around and shouting. There was other shouting. Dirt and stones started flying back at us from Dusting's feet.

'I've got one of them!' the coveralls shouted. 'Jim, quick! Come and give me a hand. I can't get him out.'

Now they had Dusting!

'Thesaurus, grab my legs!'

I couldn't even see his legs. I threw myself up behind him, and got a shoe in my mouth, then a swipe across the face.

'Hold them still!' I yelled.

I managed to grab his ankles. I was pulling down, but somebody stronger than me was pulling on the other end. Then Millicent grabbed hold of me, but it still wasn't enough. We were all being dragged up, like a human train.

'Yeeeeeooow! He bit me!'

Suddenly Dusting was shooting back down on top of me. Millicent managed to get out of the way, but I had to slide all the way back down with Dusting's shoes standing in my face.

'He bit me! The little brat bit me! Look, Jim, he practically took my hand off!'

We picked ourselves up out of the heap. There was only one way to go now — further down, into the darkness. We scurried along on our hands and knees, following the torch light. The darkness yawned in front of us. It was like a big gaping mouth, and we were heading down into the throat. Dusting's torch hand was bouncing so much we never got much more than a quick look at anything. The light jumped like a bright ball from side to side, from the floor, to the roof, lost itself, and bounced back to weave about in front again. It threw crazy animal shadows on the rocks as we passed.

We could hear a jumble of voices behind us. The echoes chased after us. The cave opened out a little and became high and narrow. We could stand up now. We stopped for a moment to catch our breath, until we saw a pale flash of light straining through the darkness behind us.

We set off again. The floor became rougher. It

was full of sudden steps up and down. Every so often we heard the men. There were muffled words, yells, thumps, and clanging sounds. The cave continued going down slowly, and became colder. Suddenly, something grabbed my hand. I jumped and tried to pull away, but it didn't let go!

It was Millicent! She hadn't said anything. She'd just reached across and taken my hand. I was getting that same funny feeling I had the last time, except then I'd only shaken her hand. This time I was holding it, feeling it. How warm, and narrow, and smooth it felt. It was smaller than mine, too. It's funny how other people's hands are always more interesting than your own. I could have gone on holding her hand for days. It made me feel better. It didn't seem as dark.

'Hold it!' Dusting said. He stopped and turned around to us. 'You two are holding hands. You're not coming with me if you're going to do that. I'll turn the torch off right now and walk ahead without you. I can't concentrate with that going on behind me.'

'But we were only holding hands!' I said.

'I hate that sloppy stuff. It makes me sick.'

We let go, and he turned around and started walking again.

'He's just jealous,' Millicent whispered in my ear.

I hadn't thought of it like that before. Perhaps

Millicent was right. Maybe he was angry just because nobody wanted to hold his hand? I reached out, and took his hand.

'*Thesaurus! What are you doing? Are you crazy?*'

He shook his hand free, as if he'd just had it in something gooey. He kept on shaking and waving it about for five minutes afterwards. He even wiped it on his pants.

'What's got into you lately, Thesaurus? Are you going through some sort of change of life?'

Maybe Millicent was wrong.

'Next you'll be wanting to walk arm in arm.'

Dusting's hand hadn't felt anything like Millicent's. Both hands had four fingers and a thumb, but that was all they had in common.

Dusting's hand felt all dirty, gritty and fat. A fat, lumpy hand. It had been like grabbing a bag full of nails.

The passage began to widen around us, and became higher over our heads. I could stretch my arms out and not touch either side. My feet turned icy cold. As Dusting shone the torch down, we saw we were standing in water up past our ankles. It spread out in front of us as far as we could see, smooth and still, like a gigantic sheet of black plastic pulled tight at the corners. It looked solid enough to skate across.

'Here, this way,' Dusting said. 'It's higher over here.'

We followed him over to the far left-hand side, where there was a ledge. We had to climb up a step to get on to it. Once we were up, we had to grab hold of anything that would stop us sliding off it again. The ledge sloped down to the pool of black water, and wound itself around a wall of rock.

'Are you sure this is safe?' I asked. 'Maybe we could try going back through the water.'

'Looks too deep.'

'I could go back and see. Do you want me to go back? I don't mind.'

'Don't you ever stop talking, Thesaurus?'

'It makes me feel better when I talk.'

'Well it doesn't make me feel any better having to listen to you,' Dusting grumbled. 'If I'd known you were just going to yak all the time, I could have brought along a radio. At least I could've listened to some music every now and then.'

'I've got one of my mouth organs with me,' I said.

'Things are gloomy enough without having to listen to you play the mouth organ.'

Dusting always makes out I'm a lot worse than I really am. That's probably because he's not musical himself.

16   A caller from the other side

THE LEDGE WENT on winding around to the left, while the water went on spreading out below us everywhere else. The further we went round, the more water there seemed to be, though we could only see it when Dusting happened to shine the torch that way. But we knew it was always just down there. The stones we kicked in from time to time made little splashes.

The ledge widened at last, and I could let go of the wall. It flattened, spread out, until finally we could leave the pool of water behind us and walk across a smooth table of rock. Then we came face to face with a dozen or more cave entrances.

It was like a dark, rocky maze. Everywhere we looked there was another cave. There were some so small we would've had to crawl on our hands and knees to fit into them. Others went up, while others went down, or left, or right.

Something splashed into the water; something heavy. It had come from where we'd just been, back on the ledge. Then there were another two splashes as loud as the first. It was them! They couldn't have been very far away to have sounded so close.

We went for a tunnel which looked like it went upwards. The water and the ledge disappeared behind us for good, and we started climbing. I felt the roof become lower, and the walls close in around us again. A little further on it split up into two directions.

'Which way now?' I asked. I had to say something. We were all just standing around staring.

'To the left,' Dusting said. 'It's this way, to the left.'

'I want to go up the right one,' Millicent said.

'Well you can't. I've got the torch, and I'm going up the left. Anyway, I've got a feeling. I can feel the vibrations on the left side.'

'What vibrations?'

Dusting started running up the left one.

'You wouldn't understand because you're not psy — uuuuh!'

Dusting had gone only four steps in before he'd hit his head on solid rock. There was no cave there.

'It must be the other one,' he grumbled.

The other cave climbed gradually at first. It narrowed, so that we had to walk in single file, then widened again to two or three metres across. It turned right and steepened. The floor became smooth and wet and I almost slipped. There was water streaming down the sides and running over the floor under our feet. I crouched down; it was easier to keep my balance that way.

Dusting pointed to something up ahead. There was some kind of pale yellow light, colouring the walls around where the passage turned a sharp left.

'Do you see that?'

'Perhaps it's a way out,' Millicent said.

'It's not a torch light,' Dusting muttered. 'Too steady for a torch light.'

It was an opening! We'd found a way out! We started hurrying faster. It was difficult to run with the floor so slippery, but I was getting better at it now. We were almost there, practically out. We turned left. The glare of the light became stronger as the cave levelled, rose up, and slid back down a little way. I was already thinking about the sandwich I was going to make myself once we got back to Melbourne.

Hang on! Dusting stopped dead in front. He dropped to the floor and scrambled to one side.

'Get down,' he whispered.

Millicent pulled me down beside her. There was a man walking towards us. The light had been coming from him, from a lantern in his hand! He hadn't made any sign that he'd noticed us. He was alone, maybe ten metres away. He took a step down, carefully, so as not to slip.

This wasn't a way out. Behind him there was just more blackness. I had a funny, jumpy feeling.

Something was telling me to turn back and run, to get out of there as fast as I could. The man still hadn't seen us. The lantern wasn't throwing out enough light.

'Who is he?' Millicent whispered in my ear. I felt her breath but I didn't answer. I didn't know.

He reached a small crest rising out of the rock. He stepped, and almost slipped over it. The walls gleamed and rippled either side of him, almost as if they were moving instead of him. But it was just that he was walking slowly, taking dwarf steps.

I could see more of him now. He didn't look all that tall; more round, and a little fat, with the sort of short legs that can only take short steps. The light was catching something shiny on his face every so often. He had glasses on.

'It's him!' Dusting murmured. His voice was thin and weak. 'He's come back from the dead.'

Then I saw the overcoat. It was the same sort of overcoat the man in the kiosk had worn. *It was the man from the kiosk!* There was mud all over the coat, still there from when he'd been buried! I felt hot. I wiped a hand across my face. I was sweating, or maybe it was just water. I couldn't tell.

'He's come back from the other side,' Dusting murmured again.

'What?'

'He's the walking dead. A zombie.'

'Who is he ?' Millicent asked again.

'It's him,' I answered. 'The man from the kiosk — that old man who served us.'

'How can it be? He's buried. Dead.'

'I know he's dead,' I said, 'he's just not buried any more.'

Millicent's mouth dropped open. She looked at me, then Dusting, down at the old man, then back at me again before she closed it.

'I can feel his presence,' Dusting whispered.

I turned back to look at the old man. He was about four metres away from us. He'd stopped walking and was looking at us, smiling. He spoke so softly, I could only just hear him above the sound of the water dripping.

'They've been looking for you.'

There were tidal waves in my stomach. It felt full of swirling currents.

'They've found your friend Max. Did you know that? He's going to be all right.'

Millicent grabbed my arm.

'Maybe he's friendly,' she whispered to me.

What was she saying? Who cared if he was friendly or not. He was dead!

'I had a feeling I might find you children here. There's a way out, behind me. Come with me, I'll show you.' He started moving over, closer. He held out a hand, offering it to us.

Suddenly Dusting screamed. He jumped up, banged his head against an overhanging ledge,

and was off, running back down. I started to get up to do the same, but I couldn't shake Millicent's hand free. She didn't seem to want to go anywhere.

'*Let go! Millicent, let go!*'

'There's no need to be afraid!' she said. 'Can't you see he's come down here to help us? Didn't you hear him?'

He'd almost reached us. I could smell something awful. It was the kerosene, and something else — a musty, damp smell. The man tried to grab my free arm.

'Nooooooo!'

I threw myself back and pushed Millicent off to one side with me. Then I tripped over backwards and landed face down. Dusting's torch was there, lying on the floor in front of me. I picked it up and pulled myself on to my feet.

'You must be Roger Thesaurus,' he said. I didn't answer. 'There's really no need to be scared.'

Millicent was kneeling between the man and me. I grabbed her by the wrist and pulled her back up to where I was but she tried to pull back from me. She didn't seem to want to come.

'He won't hurt us,' she said. 'He's here to get us out.'

What was wrong with her? I yanked her harder in my direction.

'He's dead!' I yelled. 'He can't help us!'

I pulled her further away. She began to give in, to come my way. I got her running back down behind me.

'No! Don't go back down there!' hc yelled after us. 'What are you doing? This is the way out, behind me. It's dangerous down there. It floods!'

I wasn't going to listen to a zombie. I skidded out of control and slammed into a wall, but I hardly noticed it. I got up and glanced back at Millicent. She hadn't covered half the distance I had. She was only walking.

'Millicent, hurry up.'

'I'm coming, I'm coming.'

I kept on going, looking out for Dusting as I went. I couldn't see him, I couldn't even hear him any more. For somebody without a torch, he'd really covered some distance. I reached the fork. Still no sign of Dusting. Millicent had picked up speed behind me and I could hear her clattering down over the rocks.

I made it back down to the smooth table area where all the tunnels began. The pool of black water was still there, as was the ledge we'd come around. I crouched down just beside the entrance to the cave and waited for Millicent to catch up. I heard her stop a few metres further up.

'We've got to try and find Dusting,' I puffed.

She didn't answer. I waited, then said it again. She still wasn't answering. I shone the torch back up in the tunnel. There was no one there.

'Millicent?'

I stood up and walked back. There was a rock there, about half the size of a bowling ball. It had got stuck behind another, bigger rock. I kicked it free and it went rolling down, clattering all the way. What I thought had been Millicent was really just a rock. One of us must have kicked it free up there. I walked back a few more steps and called out again.

'Millicent? Where are you? Are you anywhere?'

She wasn't. There was just me and my voice. I sat down again and listened. I listened to my heart beating, and to the plop, plop, plopping the dripping water made. That's all there was to listen to.

17   So long, Millicent

I SUPPOSE I was the lucky one. I was free, and I had the torch. I didn't feel all that lucky, though, I felt dizzy, and mixed up. I tried to work out some sort of plan in my head. I needed something. I couldn't just go on sitting there.

I was pretty certain I could feel my way back around the ledge and out to the pit again. But what would be the use of that if the men were still out there? I could wait until they went; they'd have to leave sooner or later. But what if they didn't? And what if I ran into them somewhere on the way? I didn't know. I just didn't know what to do.

I shone the torch down at my feet. One of my shoelaces was undone. I did it up, three times. My head started to swim each time I bent down, and my hands were having trouble working. I couldn't stop them from shaking. A stone skipped free of something up ahead in one of the caves, and I jumped up so quickly I practically knocked myself unconscious on a rock above.

I pulled Max's will out of my back pocket. It

was all scrunched up, like a dirty hanky. I ironed it out as best I could on my knee, wondering if it was time to open it. Then I wondered if *anyone* would ever get to open it, if it would ever be found, if *I* would ever be found.

I decided I'd hang on, and put the will back into my pocket. I already knew what I was getting anyway, or what I was going to get. Still, I couldn't help feeling curious about who got his remote-control TV. I sort of thought it might have been me. I don't know why, I just figured it that way.

'Thesaurus! Thesaurus!'

That was Dusting!

'Dusting!' I stood up and shone the torch around. He'd sounded short of breath. There was no sign of him.

'Over here, in the water.'

I ran across and knelt down over the pool, as close as I could without falling in. There was a sharp drop of at least a metre down to the water. It was too far down to reach him. Dusting was in the water up to his neck.

'What are you doing down there?'

'I'm trying not to drown.'

'How did you get down there?'

'I don't know. I forgot there was water and ran straight in. Are you going to help me out, or interview me?'

I got down on my stomach, and stretched my

hand out to him. It wasn't enough, he couldn't reach.

'Further! Can't you get over any further?'

'I'm trying,' I said.

'Will you hurry up? I can't go on treading water forever.'

'If I had a rope I could throw it to you.'

'And if I had a ladder, I could climb out myself. Hang on, that gives me an idea! Take off your windcheater, we can use that. You can throw it out to me.'

'My windcheater! But it'll stretch. Can't we use something else?'

'Thesaurus, I'm going to drown any minute. Forget about your windcheater. I'll buy you a new one, any colour you want.'

'Green?'

'Any colour you want. I'll even make it myself. Just hurry up.'

I took it off and threw it across. I held on to one sleeve, while he grabbed the other, and started pulling himself up it. He worked his way along until I could get a grip around one of his wrists. Once he could get a hand on the ledge, I grabbed handfuls of his raincoat, and pulled him up the rest of the way. He made it to dry land, and lay back on his elbows, exhausted.

'You must have been pretty scared,' I said, 'the way you cleared off so fast. You even dropped the torch.'

I handed it back to him.

'I didn't drop it, I left it for you two.'

'I thought you must have been so frightened you panicked and forgot it,' I said.

'No, I ran down first to make sure it was safe. I wanted to get away first so I could warn you.'

'Oh.'

'Where's Millicent?'

'She didn't make it,' I said.

'You mean she's still up there? With him?'

'She didn't seem to want to come.'

I tied the windcheater around my waist. The

arms were so stretched I could have worn it as a pair of pants.

'Zombies,' Dusting said. 'I've read about them. They can take over your mind like that, and make you think everything is okay. That's what he's done to Millicent, he's put her in a trance.'

'What will he do to her?'

'Can't tell. You never can with the walking dead.'

'We've got to go up there and save her,' I said.

'Not me. I'm not going up there again.'

'But we can't just leave her up there!'

'The best thing we could do for Millicent right now, is go and bring back help.'

'You go back if you like, but I'm staying until I find her.'

'Okay, I'll see you later, Thesaurus.' Dusting walked away a few steps, turned, and came back. 'All right, all right,' he moaned. 'I'll give it one hour. After that, I really leave.'

We heard people sounds coming our way from one of the tunnels, but we couldn't tell which one. We waited to hear more. Perhaps it was a rescue party. Then we heard them talking.

'This place gives me the creeps. It makes my skin crawl.' It was the murderers again.

'We'll pick them up soon, we have to. They can't keep walking around down here forever.'

I could see the torch lights shooting out of one

of the tunnels just in front of us. The beams were prodding about over the floor and sides, like long poles feeling their way along.

'In the water,' Dusting said. 'Come on.'

He shoved the torch into a pocket and started lowering himself over the edge.

'But how are we going to get out again?'

'You can stay up there if you like,' he said.

I followed him in. Ugh! It was like slipping down into cold, thin, black quicksand.

'The water must be rising,' he said. 'See, it's not as far down from the top of the ledge as it was before.'

It was a bit difficult for me to answer. I was drowning. I couldn't touch the bottom, and there was nothing to grab on to.

'They're coming over here,' Dusting whispered.

I tried turning around to see, but I was grabbed around the neck before I got the chance. It was Dusting. He had me in a headlock. He was strangling me!

'What are you doing?' I squeaked. (I couldn't exactly talk.)

'I'm pulling you to safety.'

'I can't breathe!'

He was swimming sidestroke across the water, and choking me to death at the same time.

'Just relax, Thesaurus.'

'How can I relax? My head is dipping under-water.'

What was the use of him pulling me to safety if I was going to be dead when he got me there? I struggled to get free, but he tightened his grip even more. We reached a rock ledge on the opposite side where we could hang on and wait.

Five, no, six men appeared out of the cave and walked across to where we'd just been sitting. From a distance they were just dark figures wandering about, but I thought I could recognize the man in the white coveralls amongst them. He was holding on to one of his hands. One of the others crouched over the water, and shone his torch across it, to and fro, to and fro, searching. Suddenly the beam shot over in our direction.

I felt my head shoved down, and a black, wet hole opened up around my face. I was underwater. I tried pushing my way back up, but felt the pressure of Dusting's hand holding me down. A moment later he let go, and I bobbed back up.

'I could have drowned,' I spluttered.

'Keep your voice down.'

'But I didn't have any air in my lungs. You should've said something first!'

'There was no time. Get ready to go under again.'

I looked over to the ledge. There were three of them kneeling down by the water now.

'I can't do it,' I said. 'I hate sticking my whole head underwater.'

'Just pretend you're in the bath.'

'It won't work.'

'Sure it will. Just tell yourself you're having a bath. Pretend that we're both in a bath, and you're just washing your hair.'

A bath! That was the most stupid thing I'd ever heard. It wasn't anything like a bath! I have shallow baths, that way I don't have to get wet all over. I can sit carefully and just get the backs of my legs wet. I certainly don't fill it up so full that I can't touch the bottom. Our bath-tub isn't that deep. Besides, what would I be doing in the same bath as Dusting?

'Okay, now!'

He pushed me under again, but I'd managed to grab about a thimbleful of air that time. We stayed under longer, though. It was like having a big, wet sock pulled over my head. Finally, he let me up again. I spluttered and wiped the water out of my eyes.

'It's okay,' he said. 'They've gone down into one of the other caves.'

Dusting pulled me back across to the first shelf. He was right, the water had risen. We could pull ourselves out easily now. We could hear the group of men talking and moving about in one of the caves off to the left of us. Dusting got the torch going again and we started back up the cave where we'd last seen Millicent.

Dusting was walking up too fast. I could have kept up a lot more easily if he'd shone the torch back in my direction every now and then, but he didn't. He just kept on marching up, and I kept on stumbling after him. I told him I was going to slip, and I did. I missed my step and slid down, landing over to one side. I hit my elbow, sending a landslide of stones tumbling down behind us.

'Can't you watch where you're walking, Thesaurus?' Dusting snapped.

'I can't watch if I don't know where to look,' I said.

'Ssssssh! I think I can hear them below us again.'

I listened, and heard them too. The murderers had changed direction. They'd heard me and were on their way towards us. We had to move even faster now. I felt my way up again and ran after Dusting. We passed through the narrow bit, straight into a pool of water. It was up to our knees.

'This wasn't here before,' I said.

Dusting didn't answer me. There was only a metre or so before the floor rose again. Dusting went on sprinting. There was more water everywhere up there. It was running down the walls in sheets, and raining down off the roof on top of us. We reached the bend where we'd last seen the old man, but there was no sign of Millicent or him. The shouts below were still coming up after us.

We fell splashing into more water, up to our

waists this time. We reached a ledge, crawled up on our stomachs, and kept on following the cave as it went up. It was like trying to run on wet bathroom tiles.

'There they are!' Dusting whispered.

He stopped and pulled me to one side. About twenty yards ahead we saw the old man and Millicent. They were walking hand in hand, with their backs to us. That meant they hadn't heard us yet.

'Surprise is our only hope,' said Dusting.

'I've changed my mind,' I said. 'Let's go and get help first.'

'Too late. We can only go up or down.'

Something was kicked free below us somewhere.

'I guess you're right,' I said.

'Okay, now listen good, Thesaurus, I'm only going to tell you once. We run close to the walls, so we don't make so much noise splashing. We'll just have to hope they don't hear us first. When we get to Millicent, I'll grab her left arm and you take the right. We run until we get clear.'

'But why do I have to grab her right arm? That's the one he's holding. I'll have to rub shoulders with him.'

'You know I'd grab the right arm if I could, Thesaurus, but I can't.'

'I don't see why not. You're the strongest out of us, you could—'

'You're right, Thesaurus, but this is different. I can't risk getting that close to him. Since I became psychic I'm too sensitive to some things. If he got control of my mind, there's no telling what could happen.'

We set off. We had to run side by side, and not only that, we had to run in perfect step with one another. It was Dusting's idea, to keep the sound of our footsteps down. It was practically impossible as Dusting's legs are much bigger than mine.

We'd almost reached them when I got a glimpse of the cave ahead of them. It rose steeply, then wound around to the left. The collar of the old man's coat was turned up, and he held the lamp with one hand while the other had Millicent. They turned and saw us at the last moment, but it was too late. Millicent had pulled her hand free when she'd turned around. I shot through between the two of them, grabbed her hand while Dusting caught the other. It was a bit like a relay race with a baton the size of a person. Millicent pulled back and tried to shake free of us, but we were pulling harder.

'Let me go! What are you doing!'

'Don't listen to her, Thesaurus! She's under some sort of spell.'

'You've got it all wrong. He came back down to help —'

'Don't listen, Thesaurus!'

I was going deaf from all the shouting.

'You're maniacs!' Millicent went on yelling.

'Just ignore her,' Dusting shouted back. 'She doesn't know what she's saying.'

'Let me go! *Let me go!*'

We didn't. We pulled her all the way around the bank, through more waist-deep water, and then up on to a ledge. There was no sign of the old man behind, but we kept on going. We ran up further, across a lot of loose rocks, through a keyhole gap, another step up — and we were *out*.

18   Hooray!

I KNEW WE were out. I could smell it, feel it, hear it. I could taste the drops of rain splashing against my face. I could feel the wind brushing my hair. We were in the middle of a blast of lights, spotlights surrounded us. And people! There were people everywhere, clapping and cheering. There were police, reporters, farmers, holiday makers, locals from the town, Mr Lipscombe, Mrs Sweet, and Gilbert. There were cameras, cars, vans, an ambulance, and people with ropes and shovels.

We let go of Millicent.

'You two are so stupid!' she shouted. 'What did you think you were doing?'

Dusting didn't know. I could tell by the dumb look on his face. And I knew that I didn't know.

Ms Mitchell came out of the crowd and led us across to some canvas chairs beside a trestle table. There were cups of soup, mugs of hot chocolate and sandwiches laid out all over it. It looked like somebody's birthday party. There were so many people talking to us at once, I couldn't concentrate. Some man I'd never seen before even came up and shook my hand.

We sat down. Millicent wasn't with us, but was back standing outside the cave, peering down into it. Somebody draped blankets over us, and handed us cups of vegetable soup.

'What's happening?'

Nobody answered me. They were too busy asking us if we were all right. Dusting must have told them he was all right fifteen times, and they were still asking him. Max appeared from the crowd. I didn't recognize him at first, because he must have had about thirty blankets around his shoulders. There was a nurse with red hair and a lot of teeth beside him.

'*Max!*' I started to jump out of my chair. Ms Mitchell held me down.

'Sit down, Roger, he'll come over.'

'You're okay!' I said. 'You made it! You escaped!'

'Escaped?'

'How else could you be here?'

'Hasn't anybody told you yet?'

I shook my head. Dusting was pretending not to listen.

'It wasn't like we thought at all. It wasn't anything like a murder.'

'Just a robbery, then?'

'No, it wasn't even a robbery. Do you want to guess?'

Max loves stretching things out. He gets a real kick out of it.

'They were kidnappers?'

'You're not even close. Give up? They were just plumbers. The old man from the kiosk had a busted pipe or something, and his pump wasn't working.'

'Then where was the old man?'

'Fishing.'

'Fishing?'

'And you know when we thought they were looking for the money?' he laughed. I didn't think it was all that funny. 'Well, they were just trying to find his outside tap.'

I spilled soup over myself. It burnt my leg and ran down over my pants.

'I bumped into them just after I left. I must have taken the wrong turn, because I ended up right back at the garage. They explained it all to me then. Then I took them back to the pit, and they went in to try and find you.'

'Then how come everybody is here and not there?' I asked. 'How did they know we'd turn up here?'

'This is the only way out now. The other entrance is flooded. They said if you were still alive, this is where you'd have to turn up sooner or later.'

'Why is there a nurse standing beside you?' Dusting asked. I was wondering about that too.

'She's keeping an eye on me. The doctor told her to.'

'Doctor?'

'I almost died. The doctor said another three weeks of exposure and I would have been done for. They're taking me to the hospital in a minute, probably to give me a blood transfusion. I must have lost a lot of blood.'

Max went to the hospital, and Mr Lipscombe introduced us to the plumbers. Considering they'd gone to so much trouble, they didn't look all that happy to see us. The one in the white coveralls just stood there glaring at Dusting. He had a big bandage around his hand from where Dusting had almost bitten it off.

Then Millicent came over with the man from

the kiosk. He still had mud all over him, and looked tired. One of the lenses from his glasses was missing. But he didn't look anything like a zombie now. I don't know how Dusting could have thought so in the first place.

'This is Mr Minter,' Millicent said. We shook hands. Millicent sounded angry. 'I already explained how you thought he was a zombie. He thought you two must have been mad, but I've told him you're just stupid.'

'It wasn't me,' Dusting piped up, 'it was Thesaurus.'

Millicent didn't take any notice of him.

'He felt so bad about us being lost down there, he went down by himself, and risked his life and everything,' she went on. 'You two practically knocked him over. Especially you, Roger Thesaurus!'

Dusting nudged me and whispered, 'This is what happens. Do a girl a favour, and she calls you stupid.'

'I'm sorry, Mr Minter,' I said.

'Me too,' Dusting added.

'Please, don't be sorry. I want to thank you for bringing the money back.'

'It was nothing,' Dusting said.

'No, no, it was a most commendable act. I was foolish to have so much money in the shop in the first place. You see, I'd been putting it away in that paper bag and I never thought there was any chance of getting it mixed up. So few people want paper bags now. I don't trust banks, you see.'

'Neither do I,' Dusting said.

'And I've been saving up to go on a holiday for so long, I just lost count of how much was there. Three thousand dollars.' He shook his head from side to side as if he couldn't believe it. 'Far too much for just myself,' he added, 'far too much. I could take a holiday and still have plenty to give you all a reward.'

Dusting half opened his mouth to say thanks. Ms Mitchell closed it again.

'None of the children would think of accepting any reward,' she said.

'Oh, that's a pity. I would like to do something. There must be some way I can repay them.'

Mr Minter looked disappointed. He really wanted to give us a reward. Dusting looked like he was going through some sort of pain.

What we really needed was a proper holiday after that camping trip. Especially Dusting and Millicent.

Dusting went all grumpy, and it didn't look like Millicent was going to talk to me ever again. I don't know about Max. He says he never needs a holiday.

Me? I just wanted to be somewhere quiet, safe and sunny — somewhere without Dusting, but it didn't turn out that way.

19   Surfers Paradise

'I DON'T KNOW why I went to all the trouble of getting a window seat,' Dusting grumbled. 'All I've seen is clouds. We've only been out of them for five minutes, and that was when we were taking off. The pilot's flying too high.'

We were in an aeroplane. All of us. I was with Dusting and Millicent, and Mr Minter and Max were up the front somewhere.

Mr Minter had finally thought of what he could do to repay us. He was taking us with him on his holiday, to Surfers Paradise, for a whole week. It had taken some talking.

First, he had to talk Ms Mitchell and Mrs Sweet into letting us accept, then our mums and dads into letting us go. They had to meet him and everything before they would say yes. Then Mr Minter had to promise them he wouldn't let Dusting get any more ideas about looking for gold. That wasn't a problem. Dusting hadn't mentioned gold since we'd been back from Bridgewater. If anybody even mentioned gold in front of him now, he just looked away.

But here we were, two weeks later, flying.

Max had never been on a plane before. He didn't want to come, but his mum had made him again. I'm just glad it wasn't me who had to sit next to him. It was bad enough on a bus. So far, he'd panicked three times: twice when he'd tried to get into the little compartment overhead and break out the oxygen masks, and once when he started running up the aisle towards the main cabin to ask for a parachute.

When the air hostesses were demonstrating the safety procedures at take-off, Max asked the one nearest to him to do it again, so he wouldn't miss anything.

I don't know who looked worse when we finally landed at Coolangatta, Max or Mr Minter. And I thought Mr Minter liked flying.

We were staying at a place called the *Mediterranean Caribbean Units*. The whole building was painted in red and white stripes. Growing around it were palm trees, cactus plants, and banana trees. Real bananas! Growing on trees! You could just walk right up, pick them, and eat them. You could have, if there hadn't been a sign saying:

PLEASE DON'T PICK THE BANANAS

Me and Dusting and Millicent were outside, looking at the swimming pool.

'Why is it such a funny shape?'

I was talking about the swimming pool. It was bent in the middle.

'That's called a kidney shape,' Millicent said.

'Kidneys don't look anything like that,' Dusting said. 'I've seen kidneys, and they don't look anything like that. That's a liver shape.'

'A liver shape!'

'Mr Minter might know,' I said. 'We could ask him.'

'Can't. He and Max went to sleep early.'

We'd been flat out seeing things ever since we'd arrived.

We'd been to see a marine display in the morning. They had this big fish tank about the size of a swimming pool, with gropers, turtles, sharks, and about a thousand other fish all swimming around inside it at once. I was scared they'd eat each other, but they didn't. Perhaps there was too much to choose from.

It was a lot better than Robert's fish tank. He's just got two goldfish and a couple of underwater snails crawling around in a bowl.

Right next to that pool they had another one, just for porpoises. Performing porpoises. I wish my dog could have been there. He loves watching performing animals, probably because he can't do anything himself.

The porpoises played soccer, jumped through burning hoops, danced, did somersaults in the air, and played tennis. I'll never eat another fish again.

Mr Minter looked pretty tired afterwards, and decided to have an early night, even though it wasn't dark yet. Max was sleeping because of the pills. He'd been to the local doctor already. He got sunstroke, and had to get some pills to put him to sleep. That was yesterday, and he was still bright red.

The day before we went to the Currumbin Bird Sanctuary. It's the funniest thing I've ever seen. We arrived, and there wasn't a bird in sight. Nothing, not even a sparrow. But the people in charge were giving out free food. We were each each given a plate of mushy sweet bread. Dusting was the only one who liked it, and he ate half of ours as well. It was the worst stuff I've eaten in my life. I really don't know how anybody could eat it.

Nobody did, except for us. It was supposed to be for the birds.

Two or three times a day, parrots come flying out of nowhere to have lunch. Thousands and thousands of them. And people stand around holding these plates of mush out for them. (Everybody except us, that is. We didn't have any left.)

The day before that we'd been to the wax museum, gone on a river cruise and looked into everybody's backyards, and then we'd eaten out at a Mexican Pizza Restaurant.

I'd seen more places in three days than I'd seen in twelve Christmases down at Dromana. The only thing we hadn't done so far was go swimming at the beach. We were going to do that tomorrow.

'I'm going to bed,' Millicent said.

She had the bedroom next to ours, by herself. Me and Dusting had to share with Max and Mr

Minter. I stayed around for a while, then I got sick of it, too.

'I'm going to bed, too,' I said.

'What is it with everybody? This is supposed to be a holiday, not a retirement village.'

'I'm tired.'

'I don't know how. All you've done is watch a few fish splash around.'

'I can't help it, I'm tired. I'm going to bed.'

Dusting leaned back on the banana lounge with his hands behind his head.

'Go ahead then. I've got one or two things I want to do first.'

'What things?'

'Nothing.'

I left him lying there, staring across at the banana trees.

20   Millicent wears a bikini

DUSTING MUST HAVE stayed up real late. He didn't wake up until eleven o'clock the next morning. Millicent, Max and Mr Minter were already down at the beach. I waited around for Dusting. I had to. He needed me to help him carry all his beach equipment. One person couldn't have made it down there with so much junk: one umbrella, two tennis balls, face mask, flippers, six towels, one frisbee, eighteen Phantom comics, a spare pair of thongs, one football, sunburn cream, two hats, one lilo and two pumps.

Luckily, the beach was only three blocks away.

'You must have been up pretty late last night,' I said. 'Anything happen?'

'Not much.'

'Did you go anywhere?'

'Not really.'

'But you must have done something to have been up so late.'

'You shouldn't have gone to bed so early, then you could have come along and helped me.'

'Helped you do what?'

'Nothing.'

We crossed another street, the busiest street in Surfers Paradise. We were practically the only ones not wearing foreign sunglasses. (We weren't wearing any sunglasses at all.) There were cars dawdling from side to side, shopping arcades, rides, two hundred souvenir shops all selling the same things, discos, real estate agents' signs, yellow buses, and more people in sandals and long white socks than I've ever seen before.

'Millicent's got a bikini,' I said.

'What?'

'I saw her in it this morning.'

Dusting didn't say anything. He just gave me a mean look.

'Girls look different in bikinis, don't they?' I went on. 'Sort of interesting, don't you think?'

'I know what girls look like in bikinis, Thesaurus.'

'Don't you think they look interesting?'

'I've never taken any notice.'

We found the others on the beach, just down from the surfboard hire stall. Dusting sat a little off to one side of us. He preferred it that way. He didn't want anyone to know he knew Max and Millicent.

Max had come down to the beach in his shoes, socks and long pants, so that he wouldn't get burnt again. He even had on his cardigan. Mr

113

Minter was trying to talk him into going in the water.

'I'm sure you would enjoy it once you were in, Max.'

'I can't swim.'

'Well, you could always just go in up to your knees, very refreshing.'

'My pants would get wet.'

'You could roll them up.'

'If I go in quickly, can I go back and watch TV?'

'All right,' he said smiling. Mr Minter smiled nearly all the time. 'But you've got to come back and show me wet knee caps.'

Max took off his shoes and socks, rolled up his pants, and headed off into the water. Millicent went with him, in case he ran into some trouble, or met a bully.

Dusting came over and sat with us once they'd gone.

'Say, Mr Minter,' he said, 'you know a bit about girls, don't you?'

Mr Minter cleared his throat and adjusted one of his singlet straps.

'Well, I did once.'

'I want to talk to you about Thesaurus.'

I was sitting right between them!

'You can't talk about me while I'm sitting here!' I said.

'Why not?' Dusting said. 'It doesn't concern you.'

'But you're going to talk about me! That concerns me!'

'No, it doesn't. I didn't say I wanted to talk to you, I want to talk *about* you. You can stay and listen if you like, as long as you don't butt in.'

'You want to talk about Roger and girls?' Mr Minter asked.

'Yeah, both at once.'

'Both at once!'

'Thesaurus has got a problem. I thought

maybe you could help him, before it gets out of hand.'

Mr Minter had to lean around me to listen.

'It's him and Millicent,' Dusting added. 'I think he's got a crush on her or something. They've held hands a couple of times, and he keeps talking about her all the time. You know what he told me on the way over today?'

Mr Minter shook his head.

'He told me she was wearing a bikini. You see what I mean? He must be feeling funny! He didn't tell me what *you* were wearing, or Max, or anybody else. Just Millicent. Is that normal?'

Mr Minter cleared his throat. I had a feeling he was about to speak, but Dusting started up again.

'That means he's got a bad home life or something, doesn't it? I mean it's all the same to me, I'm just trying to do him a favour. But do you think there's any chance he might grow out of it?'

'One day, perhaps, but probably not for fifty or sixty years. Once you start thinking about girls it can be awfully hard to stop. That is, if you want to stop. I never wanted to myself.'

'Oh. So he's finished then.'

'Well, I wouldn't say finished exactly. It's more like a part of his life is ending. He's never going to be quite the same boy again. He's becoming a young man, and once you begin, there's no turning back.'

116

'Why do you suppose that happens, Mr Minter? That people fall for girls?'

Mr Minter smiled, 'I've never really worked that out myself.'

'You have to sort of feel sorry for him, don't you? Thesaurus, I mean.'

'Oh, I don't know, I'm sure your turn will come.'

'I don't think so. They're just not the same as me. You can't do anything with them. It's always either too high, or too rough, or too dirty, or too dangerous, or too silly, or too hard, or too immature. They're big on that word, immature.'

'Millicent seems very capable.'

They had to stop talking then. Max and Millicent were making their way back up the beach. Millicent was helping him through the crowds. Max was limping. He'd stepped on a shell.

'Can I go back to the unit now?' Max asked.

His knee caps were wet.

'I bet you feel better now, after a dip.'

'No.'

'Not at all?'

'I enjoyed walking back, except my foot was hurting.'

Mr Minter made us promise not to go out too deep, and then took Max back.

'Don't worry,' Dusting yelled, 'I'll look after them.' He turned to me. 'Say, Thesaurus, have you got any money you can lend me?'

'What for?'

'I thought I might shoot a few tubes.'

'Huh?'

'Ride the curl.'

'What?'

'I want to hire a surfboard. Have you got any money you can lend me?'

'No.'

'Oh. I'll have to use my own then.'

Dusting walked across to the hire place.

'That costs a lot of money,' Millicent said. 'Eight dollars for two hours. Where would he get eight dollars from?'

'I don't know.'

But I had a feeling it had something to do with last night.

A minute or two later, Dusting walked back past us, dragging a sailboard. (That's like a long surfboard with a sail on it.) Millicent lent me some money and I went to get us ice creams. By the time I got back Dusting was standing up on his board, and sailing out.

'I don't care what Dusting says,' I said, 'I'm glad you came.'

'I'm glad you're glad.'

'I mean, we would've had more space to sleep in and all that if you hadn't, but I'm still glad you came.'

It was harder talking to her when there was

nobody else around. Then she did it again. She reached across and held my hand. Dusting was heading further and further out. I wasn't taking any notice of him, though.

'Do you suppose this means we're going steady?' I asked.

Millicent looked at me.

'I don't know.'

'I've never liked a girl as much as I like you. It must mean that.'

'I'll have to think about it.'

My ice cream was dripping all over my foot.

'Why is Dusting going so far out? I can hardly see him any more.'

Millicent was right. He'd become just a speck in the distance. Millicent grabbed his binoculars and looked through them.

'What is he doing?' I asked.

'He's heading out into the ocean. He's yelling something. He's leaning over. I don't think he knows how to turn it around.'

We stood up.

'What happens if he keeps on going?'

'He might reach America, one day.'

'America!'

'Maybe. If he's lucky.'

She was still looking. She made a noise.

'What's happening now?'

'He just fell off. The sailboard's going on without him. He's hit his head!'

119

'His head!'

'Quick, go and tell the lifesaver!'

I did, but first I ran the wrong way, and had to turn around and run back again. I shouted to the lifesaver on the tower.

'*Help! Help! Dusting is drowning!*'

'Who?'

'Dusting! My friend, Peter Dusting. He's out there drowning!'

The lifesaver rang a bell, and a whole bunch of them came running from across the road behind the beach carrying a big reel of rope. Suddenly there were people running all over the place. I ran back to Millicent, only she was gone. I was at the right place, our towels and everything else were still there. Then I spotted her. She was swimming out, towards Dusting. She was further than half way there. The lifesavers were just getting started.

I would have gone out too, but I'm not all that hot at swimming.

Millicent reached Dusting, out past where the waves were breaking. I could only see them in between waves. She had him around the neck, and was dragging him slowly along. They made it into the far break. The waves were crashing on top of them, and they kept disappearing in the white froth.

'This is where it gets tricky,' a man beside me said. There were dozens of people beside me. The whole beach was standing up beside me looking out.

They got past the waves, but Millicent looked like she was getting tired. She was slowing down. I think she was having trouble keeping them both afloat. Dusting's no butterfly, you know. Finally the lifesavers reached them. One grabbed Dusting, while the other helped Millicent.

Dusting was dazed when he got back in, and had to lie down on the sand for a while. It took a few minutes of him shaking his head before he could sit up. Millicent was standing around shaking hands with all the lifesavers. Once Dusting could stand up, one of them gave us a lift home.

Mr Minter was all over the place at once. He bought all the lifesavers ice creams, made Millicent and Dusting lie down, cut two dozen lumpy sandwiches, sent off post-cards to everybody saying not to worry, made three pots of tea, rang up his brother in Fiji, pulled the blinds down, wiped his glasses a lot, and got us to tell him the whole story sixteen times.

Me and Max sneaked out and went down to look at the souvenir shops. I bought a couple of things: a plastic letter-opener in the shape of an umbrella pole that said Surfers Paradise on one side and Hong Kong on the other, a pencil sharpener with its own thermometer, and a belt made out of shells.

Max bought bunches of plastic grapes for each of his sisters. He got his mum and dad a purple fur-covered toilet roll dispenser.

When we got back, Dusting and Millicent were sitting together on banana lounges beside the pool. They were talking. I'm positive I saw their mouths moving. They stopped when we went over.

'What's that thing around your waist, Thesaurus?' Dusting asked.

'It's a belt.'

'It's the dumbest thing I've ever seen.'

'I'd never seen one before.'

'Of course you've never seen one before. Just look at it. Who'd wear it?'

I looked at it. There were holes drilled through each shell, and they'd been threaded on to a piece of string. I didn't think it was too bad.

'You're not going to wear it when you're with me.'

'I like it.'

'You've got no taste, Thesaurus.'

Millicent liked Max's fur toilet-roll dispenser so much she got him to take her back to the shop so she could get one for her mum and dad as well.

I sat down in her seat. I couldn't lean back though, I had to sort of sit up straight. The shells were digging into my waist.

'I thought you'd had it today,' I said.

'They rented me a dud sailboard. It wouldn't turn around.'

'What were you and Millicent talking about?'

'Nothing.'

'It looked like you were talking from back there.'

'You must have got us mixed up with some other people. We were just sitting.'

'Oh.'

We didn't say anything for a minute or two. I spent the time with my belt, looking at the shells. Every time I looked I saw a different one. I had something on my mind, bothering me.

'It was my fault that you nearly drowned,' I blurted out. 'I was so busy talking to Millicent, I wasn't even thinking about you out there.

You'd still be out there if it hadn't been for Millicent. I didn't even notice you.'

'Forget it.'

'You're right about girls. I didn't know what I was doing. You could have drowned right beside me, and I would have just gone on talking. I didn't even care.'

'Forget it, Thesaurus. Anyway, perhaps I made a mistake about Millicent. I mean, maybe she's not so bad. She swam out and saved my life. She's different from other girls.'

Dusting said that! I couldn't think of a thing to say. All I could do was look at him.

'You know what I mean, Thesaurus? I'm just saying that compared to other girls, she's probably okay.' This was a great compliment coming from Dusting. 'Breathe a word of this, Thesaurus, and I'll pour concrete down your nostrils.'

I turned away and stared across at the banana trees. There was something wrong over there, too. The bananas had gone! There had been half a dozen bunches there before, and now they'd all disappeared.

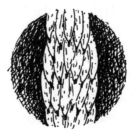

21 Yes, we have no bananas

I WASN'T THE only one who noticed the bananas were missing. The building manager came and knocked on our door later on in the night. He had a moustache and a matching bow tie, yellow teeth, fat lips, and little ball-bearing eyes. He reminded me a lot of the groper we'd seen at the Southport Marina.

Mr Minter opened the door, and we stood around watching.

'I'm sorry to disturb you at this hour.' He didn't look like he was sorry. 'But as you may or may not have noticed, we are missing our bananas.'

'Bananas?' Mr Minter hadn't noticed.

'Yes, our bananas. They were stolen last night. I've been making some inquiries today, and apparently they were first taken from the trees, and then sold door to door throughout the building. Almost everyone on all three floors has a bowl of them somewhere in their units. Not only that, but I regret to inform you that I have a reasonable suspicion that one of your children may have been responsible. The description I've been given matches that of one of your boys — the rough-looking one, with the erect hair.'

Everybody turned and looked at Dusting, who was sitting on the edge of the bed cutting his toe-nails and trying to get them to land in the waste-paper basket. He looked up.

'Sorry, were you saying something? I was concentrating.'

'Yes,' the manager purred, 'I believe I was. I was saying that a person answering to your description was identified as the one responsible for removing the bananas from our trees. We have witnesses willing to testify, I might add.'

Dusting was in for it now. There was no way of getting out of this one.

'Did you steal this man's bananas?' Mr Minter asked. He sounded a bit tired.

'I suppose I might have,' Dusting muttered. 'But I was only going to borrow one. Thesaurus said he was hungry —'

Huh? I couldn't remember saying I was hungry.

'— and so I thought that if I took just one, you wouldn't mind.'

'There is considerably more than just one missing, sir,' the manager said.

'Well, I meant to pick just the one. But when I did, the whole bunch fell down with it. Then when I couldn't tie it back up, I thought that the best thing I could do was pull all the bunches down so it looked like there hadn't ever been any there in the first place. Only then I had to think of something to do with them. So I decided that the best thing to do was to give a few to everybody. You know, sort of share them out.'

Boy, what an act! What a story!

'Then why did you think it necessary to sell them?'

'I wanted to buy Thesaurus a birthday present.'

This was December. My birthday wasn't until March.

'Nevertheless, good intentions aside, I believe you should show some recompense for your actions.'

'Huh?'

'I said I believe you should make some sort of an effort to repay us.'

'You mean jail?'

'I don't think we should have to resort to such an extreme measure. Perhaps two or three afternoons of washing dishes would be sufficient. What do you think, Mr Minter?'

Mr Minter agreed. He was looking too tired to talk much. He said good night to the manager, then made himself a cup of tea, took a Bex, and had a long lie down.

22   Afterword

THE COOK AT the *Mediterranean Caribbean* said that Dusting was the worst dishwasher they'd had there in twenty-five years. He said the only worse dishwasher had been a one-armed motor mechanic from Mexico. (And he'd only got the job in the first place because he'd been married to the boss's daughter-in-law, or something.)

On the first afternoon, Dusting broke seventeen cups, fourteen plates, five saucers, eight bowls, threw thirty-four knives and forks into the rubbish bin, and lost three teaspoons. He didn't lose or break anything the second afternoon. That's because I was doing it instead. He said that I owed it to him, for letting him practically drown the day before. And besides, he offered to pay me eighty cents an hour. He took it off the money I owed him.

Dusting still had to help the manager, though. He got the job of delivering everybody's breakfast orders. But he made himself so sick in one morning he had to spend the rest of our holiday in bed. He kept on eating a little off each tray on his way to deliver them. He ate sixteen pieces of toast, four eggs, five compotes of fruit, three packets of Cornflakes, and then drank four pineapple and seven tomato juices — just in one morning!

Millicent was famous when we got back to school. Nobody had ever saved Dusting from drowning. Dusting said it was just a figment of her imagination. He said he'd been diving for shells, and Millicent had paddled out too close and hit him on the head with her sailboard.

But it was too late. Max had told Stupid Gilbert, and Gilbert told the whole world. Besides, Millicent had been given a Special Citizen's Bravery Award medal from the lifesavers. She wore it everywhere.

Dusting only got angrier when Millicent was elected captain of the school swimming team instead of him. He'd been writing his acceptance speech since February. He was so angry he tore his bathers in half, threw his towel on the school roof, and chased Gilbert two and a half kilometres along Somerville Road.

I found Max's will the day after my pants went through the washing machine. I couldn't read it, though, it was hard enough just scraping it out of my back pocket.

I asked him who would've got his remote

control TV, and he said Mr Ericson. Mr Ericson runs the Spotswood radio and TV hire store. Max rents it from him.

Max was wrong about his mum and dad knocking down his bedroom wall to make a bigger laundry. They knocked it down to give him a bigger bedroom. It's twice as big now. The only trouble is, if you want to go out through the back door you have to walk right through the middle of Max's room. Max hasn't had any privacy since he got back. He has to do all his dressing inside his wardrobe.

Mr Minter got his car going so he can drive down and visit us on weekends. It's big and black and was made in 1938. Every time he wants to start it, he has to practically pull it to bits first.

He usually stays in the spare room at our place. Sometimes he comes fishing with me and Dusting down at Stony Creek, or else stays at home and does crosswords with my dad.

Mr Minter has taught me a lot. So far I've learnt two new card tricks, how to change a head gasket on his car, and how to knit mittens. Next weekend he's promised to show me how to do cartwheels.

Dusting bought me a windcheater, like he said he would. It's green, but it's five sizes too small for me. I can't change it either, because he bought it in a sale, and the shop doesn't exchange things bought on sale. I've tried stretching it, ironing it, washing it and hanging it on the line. I've tried everything, but it's no use, it won't fit. All I can do is hang it up in the wardrobe, and bring it out and look at it every now and then.

What else? Oh yeah, I remember! Mr Bailey has started writing a book. Millicent says he's calling it *What To Do When Encountering Aliens In the Backyard*.

Also by Max Dann

Adventures with My Worst Best Friend

When you run away from home (to see the world), miss your train, spend two hours in a cupboard full of smelly socks, tramp the city streets in the dark, and fall down an enormous hole and sprain your ankle, the last thing you want is to be pulled out by Peter Dusting, the meanest, toughest kid in school. But Roger Thesaurus survives all this, and tells the very funny story of the adventures that follow.

'A wow of a first book.' Nance Donkin, the Melbourne *Herald*

boards 0 19 5544361 0   paper 0 19 554438 2

Bernice Knows Best   *illustrated by Ann James*

Hugh had accidents. Lots of accidents. In fact, Hugh was a walking, talking accident-maker. That was until he met Bernice, the trouble-shooter — accident-prone boys a specialty. Bernice decides to cure Hugh of his clumsiness, and Hugh gets involved in the funniest and most hair-raising adventure of his life.

'Witty, superbly illustrated . . . look for the vibrating pink and green cover — it's a delight!' *The Australian*

boards 0 19 554414 5

Other children's novels published by Oxford Australia

The Inside Hedge Story   Gillian Barnett

Short-listed in the 1982 Australian Children's Book of the Year Awards.
paper 0 19 554403 X

Southern Rainbow   Phyllis Piddington

paper 0 19 554439 0

The Seventh Pebble   Eleanor Spence

Highly commended in the 1981 Australian Children's Book of the Year Awards.
paper 0 19 554356 4

A Candle for Saint Antony   Eleanor Spence

Highly commended in the 1978 Australian Children's Book of the Year Awards.
paper 0 19 550578 6

The October Child   Eleanor Spence

Australian Children's Book of the Year 1977.
paper 0 19 550548 4

Boori   Bill Scott

Highly commended in the 1979 Australian Children's Book of the Year Awards.
paper 0 19 554237 1

Darkness Under the Hills   Bill Scott

Highly commended in the 1981 Australian Children's Book of the Year Awards.
paper 0 19 554374 2

A Dog Called George   Margaret Balderson

paper 0 19 554236 3

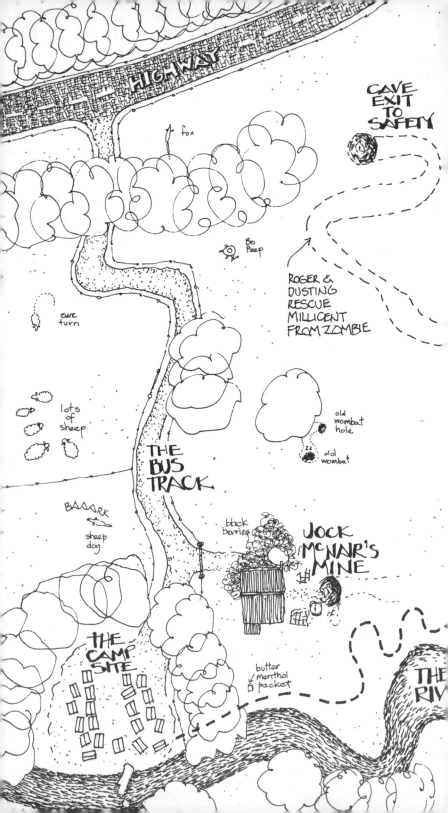